KIDS RAISED
BY THE
GOVERNMENT

KIDS RAISED BY THE GOVERNMENT

Ira M. Schwartz
and Gideon Fishman

Simon Hakim, Advisory Editor

Westport, Connecticut
London

Library of Congress Cataloging-in-Publication Data

Schwartz, Ira M.
 Kids raised by the government / Ira M. Schwartz and Gideon
Fishman.
   p.   cm.
 Includes bibliographical references (p.   ) and index.
 ISBN 0–275–96264–4 (alk. paper)
 1. Child welfare—United States. 2. Child welfare—Michigan.
3. Foster children—United States. 4. Foster children—Michigan.
I. Fishman, Gideon, 1945– . II. Title.
HV741.S367   1999
362.7′0973—dc21   98–21667

British Library Cataloguing in Publication Data is available.

Library of Congress Catalog Card Number: 98–21667
ISBN: 0–275–96264–4

First published in 1999

Praeger Publishers, 88 Post Road West, Westport, CT 06881
An imprint of Greenwood Publishing Group, Inc.

Printed in the United States of America

The paper used in this book complies with the
Permanent Paper Standard issued by the National
Information Standards Organization (Z39.48–1984).

10 9 8 7 6 5 4 3 2

Contents

List of Tables and Figures

Preface

We never intended this project to turn into a book. It started out as a study of child welfare services in Michigan. At most, we hoped to generate a few scholarly articles and reports. However, the more we delved into the child welfare system in Michigan the more we found it to be a microcosm of child welfare systems elsewhere. The Michigan system was in a state of crisis and so were the systems in practically every other state. The only difference was that the Michigan child welfare system managed to escape the scrutiny of public interest lawyers and wasn't in litigation or under federal court order for abusive and unprofessional practices.

As much as this book focuses on the problems and issues confronting child welfare, it is first and foremost a research endeavor. This is particularly evident in chapters 4 through 6, which deal with such issues as adoption and permanency, the relationship between child welfare and delinquency, and residential treatment. Because we tried to appeal to a broad audience, the research findings are presented in as straightforward and nontechnical a manner as possible. Although our findings are limited to the state of Michigan, they are similar to those that have been found in other jurisdictions.

Child welfare systems are shrouded in secrecy under the guise of confidentiality, allegedly to "protect" children. This may have been the case at one time. Now, the secrecy primarily serves to keep the public and the media from learning what is really going on inside these systems and how they are failing America's most troubled and vulnerable children. During our examination into child welfare, we found wild and exaggerated claims about the effectiveness of services designed to keep abusive and neglectful families together—claims that could not be supported by credible research. We also found examples of nonprofit organizations under contract with the government, particularly in Michigan, that avoided criticism about questionable programs because they were fearful of reprisal by state social service officials.

When research findings revealed that professionally and politically popular and aggressively marketed programs were ineffective or unable to live up to expectations, the researchers who conducted the studies were attacked by the child welfare establishment. Worse, their findings were ignored—by child welfare professionals, child advocates and child advocacy groups, national and state elected public officials, federal agencies, state and local child welfare agencies, and staff from influential and prestigious private foundations. Sadly, it was not until scandals surfaced, including deaths of children at the hands of parents who were well known to child welfare authorities, that policies were changed.

We also found that, contrary to popular belief, relatively few children placed into foster care are ever reunited with their biological families. Many, including infants and toddlers, languish in foster care for years and are essentially being raised by the government. Many of these children are kept in foster care and denied access to permanent homes, including adoption, because of national and state policies emphasizing family reunification over permanency and stability in the lives of children. We suspect many also have remained in foster care because social workers refused or resisted returning them to dangerous home environments and families they believed to be too dysfunctional to care for them properly. For this, social workers are criticized by child welfare "reformers" for being against reuniting and preserving families. More tragic is the fact that a substantial proportion of the abused and neglected children in state and local child welfare systems are in the custody of systems that have been successfully sued because they cannot provide the basic care and protection these children need. In these instances, abuse and neglect by the government was substituted for mistreatment suffered by children at the hands of their parents.

We also looked at the federal role in child welfare, including recent and past national legislation and the ideology/philosophy behind these laws. Until recently, national and state policies emphasized that child welfare systems should do two things simultaneously: protect children and strengthen and preserve their families. To the lay person these seem to be wonderful and appropriate goals. In practice, they have generated much confusion on the part of child protection workers. In some instances, attempts to balance these goals were translated by social workers to mean giving priority or being pressured to keeping abused and neglected children together with parents who, unfortunately, continued to mistreat their children. In some instances, children died as a result of these practices. Again, when scandals emerged the policies started to change.

We are impressed by the ability of the child welfare system to fight off, co-opt and resist any attempt at reform, whether reforms be administrative, legal, regulatory, or legislative. The National Commission on Children observed that "marginal changes will not turn this system around." Accordingly, in the last chapter (7), we make a number of bold and controversial recommendations which go well beyond business as usual (e.g., throwing more money at the system, hiring more social workers, providing better training for staff, or developing a new "quick fix" program).

Acknowledgments

In carrying out this project, we benefited from the expertise, thoughtful criticism, and hard work of many people. Although we cannot list all those who helped and encouraged us, there are a few we must acknowledge. Drs. Jeffrey Friedman and Chang-ming Hsieh were our research assistants. At the time they worked with us they were doctoral students, and now they are off pursuing their own careers. Based upon the work they did with us, we have no doubt that they will be very successful in the years ahead. Rosalinda Rendón, and Kimberly Osborne were our staff assistants. They performed their jobs with extraordinary efficiency, skill, patience, and good humor. They often gave us the boost we needed when the task ahead seemed overwhelming. Finally, we want to thank our families, particularly Dina and Elaine. We could not have completed this work without their love and support. We are truly blessed.

CHAPTER 1

A Wake-Up Call for the Child Welfare System

The child welfare system is broken. Worse, no one seems to know how to fix it. In its report *Beyond Rhetoric*, the National Commission on Children summed up the situation with the following observations:

If the nation had deliberately designed a system that would frustrate the professionals who staff it, anger the public who finance it, and abandon the children who depend on it, it could not have done a better job than the present child welfare system. The goals of family reunification and permanency planning remain paramount, but dramatic increases in the number of troubled families and misplaced financial incentives to the states make these goals nearly impossible to achieve. (National Commission on Children, 1991, p. 293)

The Commission concluded that "marginal changes will not turn this system around. Instead, we need comprehensive reform based on fundamental restructuring of our efforts to help troubled children and protect vulnerable children" (National Commission on Children, 1991, p. 293).

THE STATE OF CHILD WELFARE SERVICES

The public knows very little about the child welfare system, except for the seemingly increasing number of scandals appearing in the media. The system is shrouded in secrecy, allegedly to "protect children." The fact that so little is known about the system is a tribute to the child welfare establishment (child welfare administrators, social workers, juvenile and family court judges, and many "child advocates"). They have done a remarkably effective job of keeping the system hidden from public scrutiny.

While the public has been kept in the dark, there have been some very troubling developments. More than twenty-five state child welfare systems are either being sued or are under federal court order because of abusive and unconstitutional practices (National Center for Youth Law, 1993). Dozens of similar lawsuits have been filed against local public child welfare agencies.

Class action lawsuits are not the only problems confronting the system. The number of children being propelled into public child welfare systems is growing at an alarming rate (U.S. Bureau of the Census, 1990; National Study of Preventive, Protective, and Reunification Services Delivered to Children and Their Families, 1995). Experts estimate that as many as 500,000 children will be in foster care by the end of the decade, almost twice the number in such care ten years ago (U.S. Bureau of the Census, 1990; Green Book, 1993; National Study of Preventive, Protective, and Reunification Services Delivered to Children and Their Families, 1995). This extraordinary growth, coupled with the inability of child welfare systems to insure that children are adequately cared for, are prompting calls for a return to orphanages (National American Council on Adoptable Children, 1990; Morganthau et al., 1994; Lewis, 1995; DiIulio and Lindinger, 1995). Moreover, those advocating for orphanages include prominent public figures and representatives from the media (e.g., Newt Gingrich, speaker of the House of Representatives; Joyce Ladiner, acting president of Howard University, U.S. Senator Daniel Patrick Moynihan; and syndicated columnist Claude Lewis).

Although child welfare officials and child advocates claim that child welfare services are underfunded, there is a fair amount of waste in these systems. For example, more than 45 percent of federal and state child welfare dollars are spent on serving only 20 percent of the children in the system. These are children placed in residential treatment centers and group homes because they have been diagnosed as having emotional and behavioral problems. While these children may, indeed, have such problems, there is virtually no credible scientific evidence to suggest that placement/treatment in these types of institutions works or is any more effective than are other less costly and less intrusive interventions (Henggeler, et al., 1993; Scherer, et al., 1994). While the great majority of foster parents are caring and compassionate, many are not. Many are poorly trained, and others are abusive to the children they are entrusted to care for. A few exploit the system for personal gain.

Thousands more children should be legally freed for adoption than is now the case. Many couples and single adults are told every year that there are no young children available for adoption, except, of course, those with serious physical problems and abnormalities. Not wanting to adopt a child with "special needs" or to be placed on a waiting list for years, increasing numbers of these people are shelling out $15,000 to $40,000 to "buy" an infant born in another country. Yet, infants are one of the fastest growing populations in most public child welfare systems and, contrary to popular belief, most of these children are not being returned quickly to their birth parents or parent; nor are many being adopted. They are spending their childhood in foster care and essentially being raised by the government.

Almost daily, there are shocking media reports of abused and neglected children known to child welfare authorities who are allowed to stay with or be returned to their parent(s) or guardians only to be mistreated again or, as is sometimes the case, to be killed. These tragedies are calling into serious question recent federal and state child welfare policies emphasizing "family preservation" and reunification, or keeping abusive families together if at all possible and reunifying families where children had to be removed in order to be protected.

There are indications that state and federal policymakers are becoming more sensitive to the dangers children might face as a result of these policies. For example, legislation proposed by the 105th Congress, particularly in the House, acknowledged that the pursuit of "reasonable efforts" to preserve and reunify families cannot be unconditional. It should not apply in cases of "'aggravated circumstances' as defined in state law (abandonment, torture, chronic abuse, sexual abuse)" and when "a parent has killed or assaulted another of their children" or when "a parent's rights to a sibling have been involuntarily terminated" (Memorandum, Congressional Research Service, 1997, p. 3). While these legislative proposals seem logical and appropriate, they represent a major and long overdue shift in public policy, a shift toward emphasizing the primacy of the protection of children over the preservation and reunification of abusive and neglectful families.

Although Congress recently enacted a major new piece of child welfare legislation, Congress appears to be gearing up for a major reexamination of the child welfare system. Among other things, there are indications that Congress will probably take a hard look at the federal role in child welfare and determine whether federal funding for child welfare services should be folded into a block grant program to the states with relatively few strings attached. In fact, it is highly unlikely that the federal child welfare program will continue to remain an uncapped entitlement and escape from being block granted in light of the recent welfare reforms that were enacted by Congress and signed by the President.

An objective and comprehensive examination into the child welfare system by Congress will be met with mixed reactions. Some, including the authors of this book, will welcome such an inquiry, feeling it is long overdue. Others will try to prevent it from happening in the first place. If they are not successful in keeping Congress from looking into the system, they will try to prevent any major reforms from being implemented. In particular, they will advocate for keeping the federal child welfare program as an uncapped entitlement and for the federal government to continue playing a strong policy directive role with the states. However, if Congress and the administration have developed the political will to reform welfare and reexamine the policies and financing surrounding Medicare and are considering having those individuals who can afford it pay a higher proportion of the cost for their medical care, then we certainly can expect them to muster the political will to look at the federal role in child welfare.

Not all of those who will try to keep Congress from looking into the child welfare system are simply interested in maintaining the status quo. There are some serious issues at stake. To begin with, the federal government got into the child welfare business because many states refused or were unwilling to live up to their responsibilities for protecting and caring for abused and neglected children. There are serious questions as to whether the states will or are capable of doing so now. Child advocates and others will also point to the litigation in child welfare as a reminder of the limitations and deficiencies at the state and local levels. In addition, child welfare officials, child advocates, state and local policymakers, and foundations who have criticized the federal categorical funding approach to child welfare services are not so sure what might happen if Congress and the administration give states block grants along with the flexibility to determine how they will spend their federal child welfare dollars. In other words, those who, on the one hand, support giving states more flexibility to determine how their needs can best be met and how to use their financial resources more creatively are now concerned about how state and local level child welfare administrators and elected public officials will spend these funds. More specifically, they don't really trust that state and local elected public officials and child welfare administrators (who are political appointees in most jurisdictions) will spend their federal child welfare resources wisely. This is probably not an unwarranted assumption given what has occurred in the past and the current state of events.

There are also concerns that although states will have more flexibility in determining how their federal dollars will be spent, they will have fewer federal dollars to work with in the future. They are concerned about whether states will increase their child welfare expenditures if federal funds are capped and the child welfare population continues to grow. This is a legitimate criticism and cause for concern. However, as mentioned earlier, there is waste and inefficiency in the child welfare system and little doubt that existing resources can be used more efficiently and effectively. For example, it will be interesting to see if the political will can be mobilized at the state and local levels to tackle some of the sacred cows (e.g., the residential care industry) in child welfare that could result in significant long-term cost savings.

As we indicated earlier, we are of the opinion that a careful and comprehensive examination into the child welfare system is long overdue. The debates and issues that currently dominate the field include such things as the role of permanency as a desired goal, reunification and the desirability and feasibility of reuniting children with their natural parents, kinship care, the role and future of family preservation services, child protective services investigations, adoptions, and the quality of out-of-home placements. The philosophy underlying these issues assumes that children should, to the extent possible, be raised by their biological parents. One of the key assumptions behind this is that other options and alternative living arrangements fall short of children being raised by their natural parents. This philosophy has driven state and federal child welfare legislation, funding, policies, and practices for decades. It has also limited the debates in child welfare to such matters as whether one program strategy is more effective than another or what program priorities should be emphasized over others. This has had the unfortunate adverse consequence of inhibiting a long overdue debate about the real causes behind the growth of the child welfare system and whether we are really tackling the right problems.

The *National Incidence Study* (U.S. Department of Health and Human Services, 1996) indicates that the rates of child physical and sexual abuse have been declining but the rates of child neglect, a phenomenon closely related to poverty (Pelton, 1992), have been escalating steadily. Unfortunately, while the economy in the United States is booming, the rates of unemployment are down to their lowest levels in years, and the welfare rolls have dropped by 22 percent since President Clinton took office, the child welfare population is increasing. In other words, the economic boom, which seems to be lifting some families out of poverty, doesn't seem to be impacting the families at the very bottom of the socioeconomic ladder, those who are most likely the greatest sources of referrals to the child welfare system.

Focusing on poverty is important, but the problem is more complicated. The issue of income inequality and the economic disparities that stem from that, particularly as it effects the most impoverished portion of our population, seems to be an important factor. A report entitled *A Brief Look at Postwar U.S. Income Inequality* (Weinberg, 1996, June) indicates that, "Since 1968, there has been an *increase* in income inequality." It increased by 22.4 percent between 1968 and 1994. It increased by 16.1 percent between 1968 and 1992 and then jumped significantly afterwards. In addition, "The wage distribution has become considerably more unequal with more highly skilled, trained, and educated workers at the top experiencing real wage gains and those at the bottom real wage losses" (p. 3). This is further complicated by out-of-wedlock births, high rates of divorce and separation, and increases in the numbers of single parent families, all of which tend to have "lower incomes" (p. 3). Also important are the changes in the labor market. The types of jobs that are being created by the economic expansion currently taking place require skilled and better educated workers. This means that the decline in the unemployment rate primarily has affected skilled and semiskilled workers and has had relatively little impact on the unskilled. Moreover, the unskilled also have to contend with other factors, such as immigration, declining rates of unionization, and the growing use of temporary workers, all of which decrease their chances of becoming gainfully employed. The result of this is that during this country's recent and current period of economic success, the child welfare population is growing because their families are not in a position to benefit from the economic opportunities that have been created.

These, we believe, are the real and more fundamental issues Congress and the administration should focus on. They will require long-term solutions and new strategies. The other issues, such as the mission of the child welfare system, how child welfare services can be improved, what the major program priorities should be, the role of the federal government, and how the system should be financed also need to be addressed. However, as important as these are, they should not consume all of our attention and be an excuse to put aside the more fundamental issues that appear to be fueling the child welfare system.

There are signs the Congress and the Clinton administration are beginning to recognize the need to address the issues confronting the population at the bottom of the socioeconomic scale that is not benefiting from the current economic boom and the opportunities that arise from it. Unfortunately, the proposals being put forth miss the mark.

The $3 billion in additional block grants Congress now contemplates for assisting states in welfare-to-work transitions would be wasted if states and cities use it, as the legislation intends, for providing the wage subsidies, on-the-job training and job placement that are useful for the middle tier but of no use to the bottom. Though some of the money could be spent on support services, which could help the worst cases, two versions of the legislation now in Congress exclude child-care spending. Tax breaks, similarly, offer companies a marginal incentive for marginal welfare cases, but no incentive to work with the tough ones. (Milbank, 1997, August 4, p. 24)

As noted poverty researcher Rebecca Blank observes, "The rhetoric is we're really going to eliminate dependency, but it's not going to happen for the most disadvantaged" (quoted in Milbank, 1997, August 4, p. 24).

THE PROBLEM CONFRONTING CHILD WELFARE NOT NEW

In 1978, the Children's Defense Fund (CDF) published *Children Without Homes: An Examination of Public Responsibility to Children in Out-of-Home Care* (Knitzer, Allen, and McGowan, 1978). This influential book focused national attention on the child welfare system.

CDF researchers found that social workers directly involved with troubled families were under great stress. They had "impossibly large caseloads, excessive and meaningless paperwork, no time to get to know children for whom they make decisions, no time to visit families, and no training to deal with complex family problems" (Knitzer, Allen, and McGowan, 1978, p. 5). Because of the absence of even the most basic data, researchers were unable to determine precisely how many children were placed out of their homes or how many such placements could have been prevented if appropriate preventive services were available. They concluded, "The sad fact is that for many children out of their homes, there is no end; they simply grow up in the foster care—never certain of their status" (p. 25).

Even more alarming was the finding that "states are often neglectful parents—even abusive—to meet their ongoing obligations to individual children at risk or in placement" (Knitzer, Allen, and McGowan, 1978, p. 6). The researchers also found "evidence of serious and continuing abuses to children by the providers of services" (p. 48).

In 1980, Congress enacted The Adoption Assistance and Child Welfare Act (P.L. 96–272). The CDF study provided much of the impetus for this legislation. The act was intended to prevent child abuse and neglect, strengthen families in order to prevent the unnecessary out-of-home placement of children, reunify children placed into foster care with their natural parents as soon as possible, and facilitate the adoption of children in cases in which parental rights have been terminated (U.S. Government Printing Office, 1980).

Despite these lofty goals, foster care placements declined between 1977 and 1983 but have been climbing ever since (National Commission on Children, 1991, pp. 284–5; North American Council on Adoptable Children [NACAC], 1990, August, p. 43; U.S. Government Printing Office, 1990, April 4–5, p. 6). Although placements were declining before P.L. 96–272 was enacted, the legislation and the expectations of its passage probably contributed to the drop. In addition, child abuse and neglect reports rose 259 percent between 1976 and 1989. A *New York Times* article concluded that:

Ten years after the signing of a Federal law meant to reduce the need for foster care by helping troubled families stay together, foster care has grown into a multibillion dollar system of confusion and misdirection, overwhelmed by the profusion of sick, battered and emotionally scarred children who are becoming the responsibility of the public. (Barden, 1990, September 21, pp. A1, A18)

Reflecting on the tenth anniversary of the Adoption Assistance and Child Welfare Act of 1980, Congressman George Miller, a leading and unwavering advocate for children in the United States and the author of P.L. 96–272, observed that:

Ten years ago, we promised to clean up the foster care system, save money, and help children and families through enactment of P.L. 96–272. For tens of thousands of children, we didn't keep that promise, while the conditions of children and the foster care system itself have deteriorated further. Those children, and the severely complex problems that have scarred their young lives, will remain a challenge to our society for the remainder of their lives. If we do not overcome our indifference and respond to the needs of our families, these children, and those who will follow them into the foster care morass, will remain a crushing and costly burden to the United States throughout the next century. (NACAC, 1990, p.105)

THE NEED FOR HONESTY AND OPENNESS ABOUT THE STATE OF CHILD WELFARE SERVICES

On May 19, 1991, the commissioner of the Administration for Children, Youth and Families in the U.S. Department of Health and Human Services testified before Congress about the accomplishments of the Adoption Assistance and Child Welfare Act of 1980. The commissioner reported that the act contributed to such things as:

- the spread of the permanency planning concept;

- over 500,000 special needs children being adopted and receiving adoption assistance;

- reduced lengths of stay in foster care;

- fewer children in institutional care;

- children being placed in foster care closer to home; and

- major safeguards and protections being provided to all children in foster care. (U.S. Government Printing Office, 1991, March 19, p. 8)

On January 1, 1994, the Administration for Children and Families in the U.S. Department of Health and Human Services sent out a publication notifying child welfare officials and others about the availability of federal funds for the improvement of child welfare services. The announcement stated that the "goals (of P.L. 96–272) have not been fully realized" (p. 4). The document indicated that some of the possible reasons for this included:

- social, cultural, and economic changes (increases in substance abuse, community violence, poverty, and homelessness, for example) which have affected the number of families coming to the attention of child welfare agencies and the severity of their problems;

- rising rates of child abuse and neglect reports, particularly for child sexual abuse;

- a child welfare system unable to keep up with these increased demands, given constrained resources, high caseloads, and overburdened workers;

- services planning that focuses most resources on crisis intervention and too few on prevention;

- lack of services that fit the real needs of families; and

- the isolation of the child welfare services system from other services needed by vulnerable families, such as housing, employment, and substance abuse services. (Administration Children, Youth & Services, p. 4)

Undoubtedly, some of the claims made by the commissioner are accurate. Also, the reasons listed for the limited impact of P.L. 96–272 are probably accurate as well. However, neither the commissioner's remarks nor the more recent federal publication even mention the ugly side of the child welfare system. The abuse and neglect children experience at the hands of the state.

Since 1980, more than sixty-five class action lawsuits have been filed against state and local child welfare agencies. The cases, buttressed by grand jury investigations, almost daily media exposes and accounts of mishandled child welfare cases in states, give a picture of child welfare systems and services that can hardly be described as helpful to troubled children and families. The following are just a few examples of the problems plaguing these systems.

Illinois

Patrick T. Murphy, an outspoken child advocate and director of the Office of the Public Guardian in Cook County, in 1993 filed a lawsuit against the Illinois Department of Children and Family Services (DCFS). The suit alleges:

Defendants fail to place children appropriately. They place children in foster homes, group homes, shelters and residential facilities without regard to their history of sexual abuse. They also place children with histories of sexual victimization together with children known to be sexual abuse perpetrators or at risk of perpetrating sexual abuse. They fail to inform foster parents and staff at group homes, shelters and residential facilities of each child's history prior to placement. (*Katherine M. et al. v. Sterling M. Ryder et al.*, 1993, pp. 6–7)

The allegations are reinforced by specific and shocking examples of DCFS practices. The case of José and Steven is illustrative of what appears to happen to many children placed into state care in Illinois. While under DCFS guardianship, José and Steven were placed at the

Larkin Center for Children and Adolescents, a private agency with which DCFS contracts to provide residential placement for children in its care. In February 1992, José and Steven were placed together in the same room. At that time, José was nine and Steven was 16 years old. Shortly after they became roommates, Steven sexually molested José. (*Katherine M. et al. v. Sterling M. Ryder et al.*, 1993, pp. 9–10)

Steven, who was subsequently charged as an adult with sexual assault, came from a family with a long history of children being physically and sexually abused. Steven had a known record of exhibiting bizarre sexual behavior. (*Katherine M. et al. v. Sterling M. Ryder, et al.*, 1993, pp. 10–11). "Steven's DCFS records also document a history of sexual and physical aggressiveness and behavioral problems since Steven came into DCFS custody in 1978" (*Katherine M. et al. v. Sterling M. Ryder et al.*, 1993, p. 12). The suit also alleges that DCFS "knew that while José was in his parents' custody, they forced him to engage in sexual activity with his brother Bryan" and that he was "susceptible to sexual victimization." (*Katherine M. et al. v. Sterling M. Ryder et al.*, 1993, p. 10).

Another lawsuit against DCFS resulted in a consent decree. After a team of plaintiff experts investigated DCFS policies and practices, the department agreed to meet certain minimum standards of health, physical safety, and mental health care for children. The decree included specific program objectives for DCFS and timetables for meeting the objectives (Illinois Consent Decree).

Alabama

The Civil Liberties Union of Alabama, the Southern Poverty Law Center, and the Mental Health Law Project sued Alabama's Department of Human Resources in 1988. The suit alleged that the department's efforts to exercise reasonable efforts to prevent placements were inadequate, services to children in foster care were substandard, and reunification services were virtually nonexistent. The suit also alleged that the department's practices "discriminated against plaintiffs on the basis of their disabilities, and violated Section 504 of the Rehabilitation Act of 1973" (McElroy, 1991, May-June, p. 2). The suit was settled out of court in 1991 when Alabama officials agreed to reform their system by implementing specific policies aimed at promoting "placement prevention, family reunification and permanency" (McElroy, 1991, May-June, p. 2).

Arkansas

A class action lawsuit against Arkansas's child welfare system also resulted in an out-of-court settlement. The suit attacked virtually all aspects of the system. A consent decree was signed in 1992 when state officials agreed to make comprehensive reforms, including developing placement prevention programs, improving child protective services, upgrading training for foster parents, increasing the number and quality of child welfare workers, and improving family reunification services (National Center for Youth Law, 1993, pp. 3–4). Arkansas officials also agreed to have an oversight committee of child welfare policy and practice experts appointed to help monitor plans to restructure the system.

Indiana

In 1992, lawyers from the Legal Services Organization of Indiana, Inc., postponed going to trial when child welfare administrators from the Marion County (Indianapolis, Indiana) Department of Public Welfare decided to negotiate a settlement. The suit alleges that the department's placement prevention services were inadequate. The suit also alleges that the department could not guarantee the safety and protection of children placed into foster care (National Center for Youth Law, 1993, pp. 13–14).

Maryland

In Maryland, after a long and acrimonious suit over unprofessional and unconstitutional practices, state officials and plaintiffs representing children in the foster care system signed a consent decree. Despite reports by state bureaucrats claiming they were making substantial progress in upgrading the system and eliminating abuses, monitoring reports submitted by plaintiffs' attorneys charged that "significant numbers of children in foster care in Baltimore City continue to be at risk of physical and emotional harm" (*L. J. et al. v. Ruth Massinga et al.*, 1990, p. 1). Children who should be adopted "linger in care for years before their plan is approved" (*L. J. et al. v. Ruth Massinga et al.*, 1990, p. 25). In addition, plaintiffs' attorneys maintained:

• Children without medical needs are in expensive hospital placements while they wait for appropriate foster care placements.

• Siblings continue to be painfully separated.

• One hundred forty-eight (148) foster children are in out-of-state placements costing approximately four million dollars annually.

• Minor mothers who are foster children and who are able to care for their children continue to be separated from their children resulting in unnecessary family disruption and more children competing for scarce placements.

• Children stay for months in temporary short-term shelters in need of more stable or less restrictive placements to meet their needs. Others linger in institutions and other restrictive settings while awaiting appropriate homes.

• Children wait for months for placement in regular, specialized and therapeutic foster homes.

• Hundreds of children suffer multiple placements. Some children are moved daily for weeks. Others are moved almost weekly for months. Such nomadic types of homelessness damage the child's health and diminishes the child's chance to adjust and survive.
  (*L. J. et al. v. Ruth Massinga et al.*, 1990, pp. 5–6)

Some of the case histories plaintiffs' attorneys cited as examples of abuse included the following:

• Within three months after being removed from abusive relatives, #1, a three-year-old, was placed in a 60-day diagnostic center, then in three separate foster homes during the following month.

• A three-year-old, #2, is developmentally delayed and has been placed in two 60-day shelters, sandwiched around a week in an overnight foster home because there were no resources for him. He remains in a shelter awaiting a foster home placement.

- During a six-week period this summer, 12-year-old #4 was bounced from a group home to a foster home to distant shelters in western Maryland back to a foster home (against which his allegation of abuse and neglect is still pending) to an overnight foster home and finally to a relative.

- Eleven-year-old #6 was moved four times in one week during May after beginning her placements with a diagnosis of "post traumatic stress syndrome" secondary to sexual abuse. One of the placements during that week in May included an overnight with a foster mother against whom abuse and neglect allegations were pending. Finally she arrived at a stable specialized foster home where she will be able to stay.

- Fifteen-year-old #7 has severe emotional problems. He is, hopefully, now placed long-term and appropriately in a therapeutic setting. He spent his summer being bounced in and out of 11 inappropriate short-term placements in six weeks.
  (*L. J. et al. v. Ruth Massinga et al.,* 1990, p. 19)

California

In 1992, a San Diego County grand jury investigated the child welfare system and issued a blistering report. The grand jury found the system to be entrenched and highly resistive to change (San Diego County Grand Jury, 1992, February 6, p. 3). As documentation, the grand jury referred to previous grand jury investigations and media exposes that had little or no significant impact on the system (San Diego County Grand Jury, 1992, February 6, pp. 3, 10).

The grand jury's report was comprehensive and revealing. The report noted that "in too many cases, Child Protection Services cannot distinguish real abuse from fabrication, abuse from neglect, and neglect from poverty or cultural differences" (San Diego County Grand Jury, 1992, February 6, p. 4). The grand jury remarked:

It is a sad commentary that foster families who care for these children removed from their homes for neglect will receive almost twice the amount to care for this child as AFDC allots the parents. In many cases that difference would have enabled the family to provide proper care for the child without incurring the additional societal and monetary costs of the current system. (San Diego County Grand Jury, 1992, February 6, p. 4)

The grand jury also raised serious questions about how cases of child sexual abuse were being handled. The grand jury pointed out that child physical abuse is often much easier to detect and prove than is sexual abuse. "In many cases of sexual molestation, it is almost impossible to prove that it happened.   Conversely, it is impossible to prove that it didn't happen" (San Diego County Grand Jury, 1992, February 6, p. 26). However,

the way the current system operates, a suspicion of molestation, what "might have been," is sufficient to file a petition and, all too often, sufficient to sustain a true finding.   The Jury has read numerous medical reports which invariably read, "no physical findings, but history consistent with molestation." (San Diego County Grand Jury, 1992, February 6, p. 26)

The grand jury was disturbed by this and observed that "the burden of proof, contrary to every other area of our judicial system, is on the alleged perpetrator to prove his innocence." (San Diego County Grand Jury, 1992, February 6, p. 26)

The grand jury found the reunification plans in many instances to be unrealistic. "Judges and referees were observed, seemingly without thought, ordering parents into programs which require more than 40 hours [of participation] per week." (San Diego County Grand Jury, 1992, February 6, p. 25) As an example, the grand jury described the case of

a parent who had children in all four corners of the county. She was dependent on public transportation. Her reunification plan required visiting each child once a week. She was also required to attend parenting classes, daily AA, and both individual and group therapy. Coincidentally, while in foster care two of these children were sexually abused and one was physically abused. (San Diego County Grand Jury, 1992, February, pp. 25–26)

The mother told the grand jury, "They took my beautiful children and returned broken dolls" (p. 26).

The grand jury was sympathetic to the problems confronting social workers. They had high caseloads and limited resources to work with children and families (San Diego County Grand Jury, 1992, February 6, p. 19). Despite this, in an unusual display of candor, the grand jury flatly stated, "There are some misdirected social workers" (San Diego County Grand Jury, 1992, February 6, p. 21).   The grand jury heard testimony from "attorneys, psychologists, and parents that some social workers lie routinely, even when under oath in court.   There are also numerous instances in which social workers ignore or disobey court orders" (p. 21). They concluded, "the Department appears incapable of policing its own."

The grand jury was particularly struck by the fact that there seemed to be few checks and balances in the system. For example, "The courts are viewed, and appear to view themselves, as 'pro-child,' which translates to 'pro-DSS.' The courts appear rarely to demand a high standard of investigation or performance by the Department" (San Diego County Grand Jury, 1992, February 6, p. 31). The Prosecuting Attorney's Office was accused of doing a poor job screening cases. Consequently, the system gets flooded with cases that should not be processed.

There is a wide range in the abilities of counsel who represent children. "Some of them are excellent; others are marginal" (San Diego County Grand Jury, 1992, February 6, p. 33). The grand jury heard testimony that "the approved list of panel attorneys is perceived as subject to political pressure. Panel attorneys told the jury that if they are representing the child and oppose DSS, they fear removal from the list" (San Diego County Grand Jury, 1992, February 6, p. 34). In addition, "Panel attorneys representing the parents are fearful of appearing too litigious on behalf of their clients" (p. 34).

"Every client, parent or child, in Juvenile Court appears to have a court ordered therapist" (San Diego County Grand Jury, 1992, February 6, p. 36). Court approved therapists testified:

They fear removal from that list if they oppose the recommendations of the Department. Therapists testified that social workers frequently distort reports they have been given about patients. Therapists told Jurors that, as long as they are in agreement with the social worker, their reports are given great weight. On the other hand, if they disagree with the social worker, their recommendations may not appear in the report to the court. Further, therapists said that if they disagree with the social worker they may never see their patient again. (San Diego County Grand Jury, 1992, February 6, p. 36)

Utah

In February 1993, public interest lawyers filed a class action lawsuit against Utah's child welfare system. The suit alleges that "children often experience more severe harm and more disruption in their lives while in the defendants' custody than they did before placement" (*David C. v. Leavitt*, p. 2). One of the case examples cited in the suit includes a three-year-old boy named David who, along with his two brothers, "was taken into DFS [Division of Family Services] custody due to severe physical and sexual abuse by their natural parents" (*David C. v. Leavitt*, p. 4). One of the boy's brothers died in the foster home nine months later. The autopsy report revealed "the cause of death was 'blunt force injuries of the abdomen and complications'" (*David C. v. Leavitt*, p. 4). David and his other brother were removed from the foster home because of suspected abuse. "Upon arrival at his new foster home DAVID [sic] had a black eye, a severely swollen nose, bruises on his swollen penis, a handprint across his chest, and patches of hair missing from his head" (*David C. v. Leavitt*, p. 4).

The suit also contends that:

Foster children in Utah are denied the health services that are essential to their emotional and physical well-being. They are frequently moved from one foster home to another with little or no preparation or explanation for the constant disruption of their lives. Defendants provide little training to foster parents before licensing them to care for children. Foster parents are provided insufficient information about the children placed in their homes or intentionally misled about the nature of the children's problems. Case plans are incomplete and frequently bear little relationship to the problems which brought the children into foster care. Periodic reviews of the child's status are a sham. Foster parents, parents, the child, and guardian *ad litem* are excluded or just not invited to participate. The panel of reviewers, mostly defendants' own employees, merely act as a rubber stamp for agency actions, even those which are contrary to the well-being of the plaintiffs. Children who cannot be returned home to their natural parents, and for whom the plan is adoption, wait for months or even years before defendants act to place them in permanent homes. (P. 2–3)

Florida

Florida has one of the most troubled child welfare systems in the country. Prompted by a lawsuit, Florida's governor and the secretary of state's Department of Health and Rehabilitative Services (HRS) signed a stipulation in 1992 that HRS would comply with the state's own child welfare statutes. The suit alleged that HRS violated "Florida foster care statutes specifying that no child should be kept in foster care for more than 18 months without either reunification with the natural parents or initiation of termination of parental rights proceedings" (National Center for Youth Law, 1993, p. 33). In April 1988, HRS employees wrote a memo complaining that "some children awaiting placement in foster homes are being kept at an office building in Plantation (Florida) for as long as 16 hours a day without a change of clothing, bedding or proper supervision." (Bergal, 1988, April 20). In October of 1986, the *Fort Lauderdale News/Sun-Sentinel* published a series of scathing articles resulting from an in-depth investigation into child welfare services in Broward County (Schulte, Bergal and Bochi, 1986, October 5–7). The Florida Bar Association paid to have the articles reproduced in a booklet, *Suffer the Children: The Killings the State Didn't Stop*, that was widely disseminated throughout the state. Following the *News/Sun Sentinel*'s lead, the *St. Petersburg Times* (1988, December 19–23) investigated child welfare services in Pinellas County. They, too, ran a series of embarrassing stories and published a booklet entitled *When Failure Can Be Fatal: A Troubled System, HRS and Child Abuse* (*St. Petersburg Times*, 1988, December 19–23). Unfortunately, the litigation and media exposes have had only a marginal impact on the system, which operates not very differently today.

Georgia

Georgia's child welfare system does not appear to be much better. An investigation into that system by the *Atlanta Journal-Constitution* (Hansen, 1989, June 4–10) revealed:

• Overcrowded temporary shelters for abused or neglected children have become dumping grounds for children the state has no other place for and permanent homes for children it can't place. One example: In a shelter serving Atlanta, a mentally retarded 15-year-old, who openly masturbates and who is dying from a fatal disease, sits watching *Sesame Street* surrounded by toddlers; he has been at the temporary shelter a year.

- Foster care in Georgia has become a system where children are sometimes more likely to be abused than if they remain with their natural parents, and where those who are raised by the state are often considered damaged goods. One example: A 19-year-old who spent his life in a succession of foster homes had his first-born child taken from him and his parental rights severed, in part because the state believed that growing up in foster care made the father an unfit parent.
  (*Atlanta Journal*, 1989, June 4-10).

Delaware

In Delaware, child welfare officials reportedly placed a 14-year-old girl with an "unknown family." Evidently, the girl's social worker "mistakenly" assumed her client and the family knew one another (Amster, 1992, December 2). As astonishing as this may seem, it was not the only time such an incident occurred in Delaware. Child welfare workers in Delaware are unionized. They belong to the American Federation of State, County and Municipal Employees (AFSCME). AFSCME looked into these matters and concluded, "The workers did their best under the circumstances" (Amster, 1992, December 2).

More recently, the state's child welfare system was rocked when it was learned that a six-month old girl was allegedly shaken to death by her father. According to accounts in the media, "physicians at A.I. duPont Hospital for Children reported that the child, then 4 months old, had suspicious bruises on her face (*The News Journal*, March 12, 1998, pp. 1 and 11). Staff from the Division of Family Services claim the case was assigned to be investigated by "an overworked and inexperienced" worker who only made telephone contact with the family (*The News Journal*, April 3, 1998). The child was left with the mother on the promise that she would keep the father away from the child. Obviously, the mother couldn't keep her promise. The worker is no longer employed by the state and, of course, state officials were upset over the fact that the judge who heard the case ordered that the proceedings be open to the public. While state bureaucrats were worried about maintaining the "confidentiality" of the case the judge seemed more interested in penetrating the wall of confidentiality that protects the system.

Washington, DC

If our nationally elected public officials really want to get a firsthand picture of what the child welfare industry is like, particularly in our large urban areas, they need look no further than Washington, D.C. Long recognized as one of the most notorious and chaotic child welfare systems in the country, it reached a new low when a study found that "one of every four foster children is missing, and one in 10 is in an unlicensed or crowded facility" (Harriston, 1992, August 6). A lawyer for the American Civil Liberties Union speculated, "It may be these children are runaways, it may be they are in the streets, they may be in detention centers, [however,] we do not believe management in the department knows where the children are" (quoted in Harriston, 1992, August 6).

In 1991, Federal District Court Judge Thomas F. Hogan "held that the Washington, D.C. child welfare system violated almost every aspect of applicable federal and District law, the U.S. Constitution, and all reasonable professional standards." Judge Hogan further "charged that the system was ineptly managed, that the administration of former D.C. Mayor Marion Barry had been indifferent to the plight of foster children and that the evidence presented in the case was 'nothing less than outrageous'" (McElroy, 1991, May-June, p. 1).

New York

New York City's child welfare system has been under attack for decades. Despite the enormous intellectual and financial resources concentrated in that city, no mayor, commissioner of child welfare services or anyone else has been able to bring the system under control. In the past 20 years, there have been at least four dozen studies, audits, reviews, analyses, and evaluations of the perceived disarray in the City's child welfare policies and programs. Indeed, analyzing the City's child welfare agency has become a veritable industry in itself. Numerous boards, committees, and commissions have been formed by several Mayors, the Courts, the City and State Comptrollers, Borough Presidents, the Public Advocate, the City Council, other officials and non-government entities to study, monitor and/or reform all or parts of the system. The recommendations of these bodies and reports are strikingly similar. Recurring themes include:

- all service delivery and foster care placements should be decentralized and community-based;

- staff qualifications and salary should be adequate to attract and retain capable, dedicated personnel;

- caseloads are too high to do quality work;

- staff training should be more rigorous and more extensive;

- better quality supervision is needed;

- there should be distinct, clear differentiation of the roles and responsibilities of protective/investigative workers and those who are responsible for long term case management;

- excessive and redundant paperwork should be eliminated and integrated, computerized systems put into place; and

- confidentiality laws should be eased.

> Although the very same issues and solutions have been repeatedly
> presented, only a few of the recommendations have actually been adopted;
> regardless of who wrote them or when, the reports have been relegated to
> the bookshelves. (*Protecting the Children of New York: A Plan of Action for
> the Administration for Children's Services*, The Honorable Rudolph W.
> Giuliani, Mayor of New York City, Nicholas Scoppetta, Commissioner,
> December, 1996. pp. 54-55).

New Jersey

New Jersey's child welfare system is just about as troubled and neglected
as any in the country. Evidently, it is a system that was improved and made
some significant advances but has suffered from years of neglect and
inattention. This too, unfortunately, is often the case. Sadly, a recent
Governor's Blue Ribbon Panel on Child Protection Services reported that:

> While vestiges of New Jersey's once strong child welfare system remain, the
> pattern of fluctuating fiscal and political priorities has taken a heavy toll. It
> is clear that the system has been seriously weakened by the cumulative
> effects of a decade of relative inattention and minimal maintenance. As a
> consequence, the state's child protection system, particularly the core
> element represented by DYFS (Division of Youth and Family Services),
> reached a state of crisis. Serious deficiencies in staffing, service resources
> and program capacity were apparent and demanded immediate responses.
> The general morale of people working within the system dropped to a
> dangerously low level, contributing to a pervasive lack of community
> confidence and reducing the division's response to a crises mode of
> intervention (*Governor's Blue Ribbon Panel on Child Protection Services*,
> Final Report, February 20, 1998. p. 1-2).

The panel concluded that "The overall capacity of New Jersey's child
welfare system has been seriously damaged by years of neglect" and that "the
current foster care model does not adequately address either the needs of
children coming into care or the overall needs of our child welfare system"
(Ibid., pp.1-4). And, in a remarkably candid statement, the panel pointed out
that "Insufficient safeguards exist to assure that children are not actually
suffering harm within the foster care system" (Ibid., pp. 1-4). They also found
that the system falls far short of the mark with respect to helping older children
make the transition from the child welfare system to the real world when they
reach the age of majority (Ibid., pp. 1-4).

ADDRESSING THE CRISIS IN CHILD WELFARE

The problems confronting child welfare are far broader than the
immediate crisis confronting child welfare agencies (i.e., high rates of abuse

and neglect reports, increasing numbers of children being placed into substitute care, overburdened and ill-trained staff, financial constraints, misdirected financial incentives and poor management). The broader problems are rooted in poverty, increasing pressures on the family, intolerable levels of domestic violence, high rates of teen pregnancy, lack of affordable housing, widespread availability and use of illegal drugs, and inadequacies in our systems of public education and health care (Testa, 1992). While it may take decades to address these broader social ills, we must not delay in taking the necessary interim measures needed to upgrade our systems of child welfare services. This is, in fact, what Congress hopes will occur as a result of the recently enacted Adoption and Safe Families Act of 1997.

While the attention Congress is giving to child welfare is encouraging, we must recognize that federal legislation, no matter how enlightened and broadly supported, is clearly not enough to reform the child welfare system. The aftermath of the popular and broadly supported Adoption Assistance and Child Welfare Act is proof of this. In addition, it doesn't even appear that federal court decisions and consent decrees are able to reform child welfare systems and ensure appropriate treatment of children. This suggests the need to rethink our approaches and strategies for reform as well as the goals and purposes of the system.

Unfortunately, legislative proposals being considered by Congress are not driven by accurate and policy-relevant data. This is a long-standing problem because "the child welfare area is characterized by a severe lack of national data" (U.S. Government Printing Office, 1992, July 22). The national data is derived from the states, whose information systems are obsolete, incomplete, confusing, and unreliable. In addition, despite the billions in federal, state, and local dollars that have been poured into state and local child welfare services during the past decade, there has been remarkably little research and development to guide policymakers and practitioners. As stated above, we don't know how many children are being propelled into child welfare systems each year, and we know even less about them and their experiences once the government has assumed responsibility for their care and treatment.

AN INSIDE LOOK INTO MICHIGAN'S CHILD WELFARE SYSTEM

There were no fewer than six studies of Michigan's child welfare system by prestigious commissions and task forces between 1895 and 1992. The studies contain more than 250 recommendations for improving the system. Despite these studies, "the system remains expensive and chaotic" (Abbey, 1993, January, p. 1).

As part of our research, we conducted an in-depth study of what happens to children placed into the child welfare system in the state of Michigan. Because the Michigan Department of Social Services, renamed the Family Independence Agency (FIA), is an umbrella human services organization, the child welfare system includes abused/neglected children and delinquents.

Our findings are provocative and, in some instances, counter-intuitive. More significantly, they provide important policy insights for elected public officials and child welfare professionals in Michigan. We also believe they will help inform policy discussions about how to address the problems confronting child welfare nationally.

Our data is derived from the FIA Children's Services Management Information System (CSMIS). FIA provided the data set to the University of Michigan School of Social Work to use in scholarly research studies. CSMIS is an event-driven administrative information system that includes descriptive data on children placed into Michigan's child welfare system. (All identifying information was eliminated to preserve confidentiality.) It includes information about changes in a child's legal status and living arrangements throughout his or her entire career with the system.

An interdisciplinary team of researchers from the Center for the Study of Youth Policy at the University of Michigan's School of Social Work restructured and cleaned the data set so it could be used for research purposes. In particular, the data set was reorganized so that studies could be completed on child welfare trends and the child welfare and delinquency career patterns of children. The research for this book was derived from approximately 100,000 cases of children placed out of their homes between January 1, 1980 and March 31, 1992.

REFERENCES

Abbey, J. M. (1993, January). *Chorus: Themes for Michigan's child welfare system. (A decade of analysis)*. Detroit: The Skillman Foundation.

Administration for Children's Services. (1996, December). *Protecting the children of New York: A plan of action for the administration for children services.* The Honorable Rudolph W. Giuliani, Mayor of New York City, and Nicholas Scoppetta, Commissioner, pp.54-55.

Amster, S. E. (1992, December 2). Foster priorities reviewed: Home placement under scrutiny. *Delaware News Journal*, p. A1.

Atlanta Journal. (1989, June 4–10). Something has to be done about Georgia's abuse of children. In *Suffer the children. Atlanta Journal-Constitution.*

Barden, J. C. (1990, September 21). Foster care system reeling, despite law meant to help. *New York Times*, pp. A1, A18.

Bergal, J. (1988, April 20). HRS accused of gross neglect: Staff internal memo decries leaving disturbed youths in office building. *Fort Lauderdale News*, pp. 1B, 5B.

David C. v. Leavitt, No. 93–C–206W. (U.S. District Court, Utah, 1993, February 25).

DiIulio, J. J., and Lindinger, L. G. (1995, January 8). Orphanages: Safe, stable havens for "at-risk" kids. *Philadelphia Inquirer*, p. C7.

Ford, M., and Kroll, J. (1990, November). *Challenges to child welfare: Countering the call for a return to orphanages.* (Research Brief #1). St. Paul, MN: North American Council on Adoptable Children.

Goldman, H., and Woodall, M. (1989, December 27–29). Children with no place to go. Children of crack. Children without parents. *Philadelphia Inquirer*, pp. 1-A, 6-A, 7-A.

Governor's Blue Ribbon Panel on Child Protection Services. (1998, February 20). Final Report, p. 1-2.

Green Book. (1993). *Background material and data on major programs within the jurisdiction of the Committee on Ways and Means.* Washington, DC: U.S. Government Printing Office.

Hansen, J. O. (1989, June 4–10). A home is no refuge for abused youngsters. In *Suffer the children. Atlanta Journal-Constitution,* pp.1–3.

Harriston, K. A. (1992, August 6). D. C. foster children are missing: Sampling of cases shows "absconders." *Washington Post,* pp. C1, C5.

Henggeler, S. W.; Melton, G. B.; Smith, L. A.; Schoenwald, S. K.; and Hanley, J. H. (1993). Family preservation using multisystemic treatment: Long-term follow-up to a clinical trial with serious juvenile offenders. *Journal of Child Family Studies,* 2, 283–93.

Illinois Consent Decree. District Court for the Northern District of Illinois Eastern Division, *B.H. et al. v. Sue Sutter,* No. 88 C 5599.

Katherine M. et al. v. Sterling M. Ryder et al., No. 93CH–001861 (Jury Demand in the Circuit Court of Cook County, Illinois. County Department, Chancery Division, 1993).

Knitzer, J., Allen, M. L., and McGowan, B. (1978). *Children without homes: An examination of public responsibility to children in out-of-home care.* Washington, DC: Children's Defense Fund.

Lewis, C. (1995, July 12). We could use more orphanages. *Philadelphia Inquirer,* p. A1.

L. J. et al. v. Ruth Massinga et al., No. JH–84–4409. (U.S. District Court, Maryland, 1990, September 5).

McElroy, P. (1991, May-June). New developments in foster care litigation: Federal court terms D.C. foster care system "outrageous." *Youth Law News, 12*(3), 1, 6–10.

Memorandum (1997, May 6). Congressional Research Service, Library of Congress. pp. 1–22.

Milbank, D. (1997, August 4). Under the underclass. *The New Republic, 217*(5), 20–24.

Morganthau, T.; Springen, K.; Smith, V. E.; Rosenberg, D.; Beals, G.; Bogert, C.; Gegax, T. T.; and Joseph, N. (1994, December 12). The orphanage. *Newsweek,* pp. 28–32.

National Center for Youth Law. (1993). *Foster care reform litigation docket 1993.* San Francisco: Author.

National Commission on Children. (1991). *Beyond rhetoric: A new American agenda for children and families.* (Final Report). Washington, DC: U.S. Government Printing Office.

National Study of Preventive, Protective, and Reunification Services Delivered to Children and Their Families. (1995). *Preliminary Findings.* Washington, DC: Westat and James Bell Associates, Inc.

North American Council on Adoptable Children (NACAC). (1990, August). *The Adoption Assistance and Child Welfare Act of 1980 (Public Law 96–272). The first ten years.* St. Paul, MN: Author.

Pelton, L. H. (1992). A functional approach to reorganizing family and child welfare interventions. *Children and Youth Services Review, 14*(3–4), 289–303.

St. Petersburg Times. (1988, December 19–23). *When failure can be fatal: A troubled system, HRS and child abuse.* Tallahassee: Florida Center for Children and Youth.

San Diego County Grand Jury. (1992, February 6). *Families in crisis.* (Report No. 2). San Diego, CA: Author.

Scherer, D. G.; Brondino, M. J.; Henggeler, S. W.; and Melton, G. B. (1994). Multisystemic family preservation therapy: Preliminary findings from a study of rural and minority serious adolescent offenders. Special Series: Center for Mental Health Services Research Projects. *Journal of Emotional & Behavioral Disorders, 2*(4), 198–206.

Schulte, F.; Bergal, J.; and Bochi, K. (1986, October 5–7). Suffer the children: The killings the state didn't stop. *Fort Lauderdale FL News/Sun-Sentinel.*

Spar, K. (1993, March 24). *Child welfare and foster care: Issues in the 103d Congress.* Washington, DC: Congressional Research Service.

Tatara, T. (1993). *Characteristics of children in substitute and adoptive care.* Washington, DC: American Public Welfare Association.

Testa, M. (1992). Conditions of risk for substitute care. *Children and Youth Services Review, 14*(6), 17–36.

U.S. Bureau of the Census. (1990). *Current population reports.* (Series P 25). Washington, DC: U.S. Government Printing Office.

U.S. Department of Health and Human Services (1996). The third national incidence study of child abuse and neglect. Washington, DC: U.S. Government Printing Office.

U.S. Government Printing Office. (1980). The Adoption Assistance and Child Welfare Act of 1980. (P.L. 96–272. H.R. 3439, 94. Stat. 500, June 17, 1980). Washington, DC: Author.

U.S. Government Printing Office. (1990, April 4–5). *Federally funded child welfare, foster care, and adoption assistance programs* (Serial 101–90). Hearings before the Subcommittee on Ways and Means, House of Representatives. Washington, DC: Author.

U.S. Government Printing Office. (1991, March 19). *State of the nation's child welfare system* (Serial 102–3). Hearing before the Subcommittee on Human Resources Committee on Ways and Means, House of Representatives. Washington, DC: Author.

U.S. Government Printing Office. (1992, July 22). *The Family Preservation Act of 1992* (H.R. 3603). Report of the Committee on Ways and Means, House of Representatives, Washington, DC: Author.

U.S. Senate. Committee on Finance. (1990, September). *Foster care, adoption assistance, and child welfare services.* Washington, DC: U.S. Government Printing Office.

Weinberg, D. H. (1996, June). A brief look at postwar U.S. income inequality. *Current Population Reports.* Washington, DC: U.S. Bureau of the Census.

Wulczyn, F. H., and Goerge, R. M. (1992). Foster care in New York and Illinois: The challenge of rapid change. *Social Service Review, 66*(2), 278–94.

CHAPTER 2

Child Welfare Reform: An Elusive Goal

Federal, state, and local elected public officials, child welfare professionals, child advocates, foundation staffers, and academics have been searching for the magic formula for reforming child welfare systems for decades. They have tried legislation, regulation, and litigation. They have studied child welfare services, developed new programs, and thrown billions of dollars at the system. Although the impact of these efforts has not been carefully and systematically examined, one would be hard pressed to make the case that they've dramatically improved the quality of services for children and families.

The sad fact is that no state or county has a model child welfare system. Child welfare systems are bursting at the seams with increasing numbers of vulnerable, maltreated, and troubled children. As discussed in chapter 1, many of these systems seem incapable of providing the care and protection needed by children placed in their custody. More telling is the fact that no child welfare professional, child advocate, or elected public official who has even a passing familiarity with the state of child welfare services would prefer or allow his or her own child or children to be placed into the custody of a public child welfare agency if there were any reasonable option (e.g., parents, other relatives, or friends).

WHY HAVEN'T THE ATTEMPTS TO REFORM CHILD WELFARE SERVICES WORKED?

There are many reasons why child welfare systems have been difficult to change or reform. For openers, no one knows what a reformed child welfare system should look like. There's a lot of rhetoric about reforming child welfare systems and services on the part of child advocates, private foundation staffs, and child welfare professionals, but there is no consensus or general understanding about what a model child welfare system is. Also, there is no state or county in the country that has a child welfare system that can be pointed to or referred to as a model for others to emulate. There are a few innovative and interesting strategies being implemented, such as in Los Angeles County under the leadership of Pete Digre, but these approaches need to be carefully studied to determine their impact and implications.

There are child welfare standards. The most widely recognized professional standards in the field are the ones developed by the Child Welfare League of America (CWLA). The standards encourage adherence to the "best practices" in the field and reflect the consensus of opinion of leading child welfare practitioners and academics. Unfortunately, the standards are not rooted in research and do not reflect performance outcomes. They are mainly process oriented. While they may reflect the best and most current professional thinking, they contain all of the flaws encountered when ideas and recommendations are based upon "practice wisdom," professional experiences and preferences, and anecdotal data. While adherence to such standards may result in the development of humane and efficient systems with all the trappings of professionalism, they may not necessarily result in significantly improved outcomes for children and families.

Child welfare services are not a priority for most governors and state legislators. Although child welfare services are big ticket items in states, state and local elected public officials tend to be more concerned with such issues as crime, economic development, transportation (building and maintaining roads and making sure highways are cleared during the winter), controlling Medicaid costs, taxes, and education. They generally pay little attention to child welfare services until scandals surface in the media and class action lawsuits are filed.

Child welfare reform efforts tend to be simplistic and not carefully thought through. For example, one of the major goals of the federal Adoption Assistance and Child Welfare Act of 1980, more commonly referred to as P.L. 96–272, was to prevent the out-of-home placement of abused and neglected children (P.L. 96–272, 1980). As a result, and in order to keep federal child welfare funds flowing into their states, child welfare administrators and practitioners turned their attention to trying to keep vulnerable and at risk children together with the parents and guardians who abused and neglected them. If they had to be placed into foster care, they were to be kept there for as short a period as possible and returned to their parents as soon as it was safe to do so. With the exception of the extraordinary focus on responding to child maltreatment complaints and conducting child protective service investigations, this policy, more popularly known as "family preservation," gradually grew to virtually dominate child welfare services throughout the decade of the 80s. With the enactment of the Family Preservation and Support Act in 1993 and the commitment of $1 billion in federal funds for its implementation, family preservation continues to be one of the few relatively new major policy initiatives of the child welfare system.

Senator Daniel Patrick Moynihan, former chairman of the powerful Senate Finance Committee and one of the country's leading experts on welfare issues, suspected that family preservation services were a boondoggle. While he and his colleagues on the Senate Finance Committee were struggling to put together a national deficit reduction package, Clinton administration officials kept pressuring him to fund various social programs. His "favorite was something called "family preservation," yet another categorical aid program which amounted to a dollop of social services and a press release for some subcommittee chairman" (Moynihan, 1996, p. 47). He noted that "For three decades [he] had been watching families come apart in our society; now was being told by seemingly everyone on the new [Clinton] team that one more program would do the trick" (Moynihan, 1996, p. 47).

Moynihan was so troubled by the family preservation program that he expressed his reservations in a letter to Dr. Laura D'Andrea Tyson, who, at the time, was the chairman of the President's Council on Economic Advisors. He wrote:

Dear Dr. Tyson:

You will recall that last Thursday when you so kindly joined us at a meeting of the Democratic Policy Committee you and I discussed the President's family preservation proposal. You indicated how much he supports the measure. I assured you I, too, support it, but went on to ask what evidence was there that it would have any effect. You assured me there were such data. Just for fun, I asked for two citations.

The next day we received a fax from Sharon Clied of your staff with a number of citations and a paper, "Evaluating the Results," that appears to have been written by Frank Farrow of the Center for the Study of Social Policy here in Washington and Harold Richman at the Chapin Hall Center at the University of Chicago. The paper is quite direct: "Solid proof that family preservation services can effect a state's overall placement rates is still lacking." (Moynihan, 1996, p. 48)

Moynihan also noted that Peter Rossi, concluded in a paper he authored in 1992 that there was no compelling evidence to determine whether or not family preservation worked (Moynihan, 1996, p. 48). Then, with extraordinary candor, Moynihan concluded by saying:

I write you at such length for what I believe to be an important purpose. In the last six months I have been repeatedly impressed by the number of members of the Clinton administration who have assured me with great vigor that something or other is known in an area of social policy which, to the best of my understanding, is not known at all. This seems perilous. It is quite possible to live with uncertainty, and with the possibility, even the likelihood that one is wrong. But beware of certainty where none exist. Ideological certainty easily degenerates into an insistence upon ignorance. (p. 49)

Richard Gelles, who has studied the family preservation movement in the United States, observed that:

Although state and local agencies and service providers believed in the need for and the effectiveness of family preservation programs, the expansion of the concept of family preservation and the growing support for the programs, culminating in the $1 billion commitment of federal funds in 1993, could not have been achieved without the support, financial and otherwise, of two large and influential foundations. The Edna McConnell Clark Foundation in New York City and the Annie E. Casey Foundation in Baltimore, played crucial roles in the selling, or overselling, of family preservation." (Gelles, 1996, p. 134)

Gelles continued:

Both foundations marketed family preservation with a near-religious zeal and substantial support. They funded start-up and demonstration programs and then promoted them by claiming they proved that a substantial number of placements could be prevented at little risk to children and that children would benefit because family bonds would be maintained and strengthened.

Between 1984 and 1994 the Clark Foundation spent an estimated $4 million a year relentlessly promoting family preservation. It funded a 1992 Bill Moyers TV special on family preservation that presented a glowing view of the programs and their philosophy. Here, Moyers and Clark said, was the silver bullet that could protect children and support families. The Clark Foundation and the Casey Foundation became the official repositories of expertise and data on family preservation. State, local, and federal agencies and officials (including presidential advisers) relied on the two foundations for their evaluation data in support of family preservation.

The foundations as well as other interested parties chose to filter out criticism and data that contradicted claims about the effectiveness of family preservation.

When the believers are foundations who can invest millions of dollars each year in touting the programs and when the critics are academic who merely publish their research results in scholarly journals, the outcome is entirely predictable. State and local agency heads, legislators and legislative aides, governors and presidential administrations were told about the unqualified successes of family preservation and the tremendous cost savings. The skeptics and critics were either unknown or cast as merely academic gadflies. (Gelles, 1996, pp. 134–5).

Not surprisingly, the family preservation policy thrust has proven to be extremely controversial. The research and knowledge needed to clearly identify families whose children were at risk of placement was lacking. Consequently, intensive and expensive treatment resources have been indiscriminately deployed in child welfare agencies. Families where there was little or even no risk of having a child removed from home were just as likely to receive intensive placement prevention services as families where the risk was moderate or high. In some jurisdictions, "family preservation" came to mean trying to prevent placements and keep children with their families almost at all costs. This resulted in some children being kept in dangerous environments when they should have been removed for their own safety and protection. As could have been predicted, stories surfaced in the media about infants and young children who died at the hands of their parents, parents who were often known to child welfare authorities and had a history of mistreating their children.

For example, it was reported in the *New York Times* that:

In an eight-day period this spring, three small children in Connecticut died at the hands of adults they knew.

Outraged and revolted, particularly by the rape and fatal assault of 9-month old Emily Hernandez, Connecticut abruptly changed the way it handled child abuse cases. Since then, the state has become far more aggressive about removing abused children from their parents and placing them in foster care. Connecticut officials have shifted their focus from the preservation of families, backing away from the philosophy that governs child welfare in at least 35 other states, including New York and New Jersey. (McLarin, 1995, July 30)

While the policy of "family preservation" sounded good and had the backing of many child welfare professionals, child advocates and child advocacy organizations, the federal government and a few influential private foundations, it was not rooted in any known theory or body of credible research. There were testimonials that "family preservation" programs worked and reports of extraordinary success in keeping troubled families together. However, these claims were largely based on studies with flawed designs (Rossi, 1991). Nonetheless, some of the more strident advocates of family preservation services believe that almost any of the problems families face can be corrected with the right "mix" of therapy and social services. The premise is that abusive parents are victims themselves, and their behavior toward children is a consequence of circumstances and environment and not part of the character of the abuser. In addition, family preservation was appealing because it supported the virtually unchallenged ideology by conservatives and liberals that the best place to raise a child is in his or her home, almost regardless of the possible danger. It supported the deeply held belief that the family unit is sacred and needs to be saved and maintained almost at all costs. It inadvertently reinforced the notion that children are, indeed, the property of their parents, who can do whatever they wish with them.

Despite this, as many of us have noted, there is no compelling scientific evidence that family preservation programs result in substantial reductions in out-of-home placements or that they are any more effective than traditional approaches used by child welfare agencies. There is also no satisfactory and reliable method for identifying those families who might be amenable to intensive family preservation interventions. This means that, absent such tools, children have been, and continue to be, left in harm's way under the progressive sounding, but substantively bankrupt, policy rhetoric of family preservation (Gelles, 1996; Schuerman, Rzepnicki, and Littell, 1994). There is also no compelling scientific data that such services even prevent future incidents of abuse or neglect.

In addition, many children who were removed from their families and placed into foster care were kept in the child welfare system for years because of the undying hope that they would eventually be returned to their families. One of the fastest growing populations coming into child welfare systems are infants (NACAC, 1990; Goerge, Wulczyn, and Harden, 1993; Schwartz, Ortega, Fishman, and Guo, 1996; Schwartz, Ortega, Guo, and Fishman, 1994; Wulczyn and Goerge, 1992). Contrary to popular belief, many of these infants are not being returned quickly to their birth parent or parents or being adopted. Instead, they are spending their childhood being raised by the government. For example, a recent study by the Chapin Hall Center for Children indicates that the median length of stay in foster care is significantly higher for infants than it is for other age groups in the states of Michigan, Illinois, California, New York, and Texas (Goerge, Wulczyn, and

Harden, 1995).

In many instances, social workers know there may be little or no possibility these young children can be reunited with their natural parents. Oftentimes, the birth mother is a single, young, crack-addicted teenager who may or may not be receiving drug treatment and other needed health, social, vocational, and educational services. However, the intense pressure to preserve families by reuniting children with their birth parent or parents, coupled with the reluctance on the part of juvenile and family court judges to terminate parental rights because of a small number of botched adoption cases and fears about trampling on the rights of birth parents, are keeping many children from being freed for adoption. More tragic, if these children were available for adoption, particularly while they were still infants and toddlers, it would dramatically reduce the number of individuals and couples paying exorbitant amounts of money to adopt a child from abroad.

The overemphasis on "family preservation" indirectly contributed to another problem. It diverted the attention of child welfare administrators and policymakers away from the need to improve the infrastructure of child welfare systems. As pointed out earlier, many of these systems are under legal attack because they can not guarantee the health, safety, and treatment of the children placed into their care. There is a critical need to improve efforts to recruit, screen, train, supervise, assist, and reward foster parents. The training and supervision of child welfare workers needs to be improved. There is also a critical need to increase substantially the level and quality of services to children in foster care. There are serious questions about the extent to which this occurred while child welfare agencies were scurrying to develop family preservation services.

A CLOSER LOOK AT FAMILY PRESERVATION

Family preservation services warrant more careful examination because the concept has become so dominant and well accepted in child welfare policy, service delivery, and advocacy circles. The very fact that family preservation services have achieved such prominence in the field despite the scant and inconclusive evidence that such services prevent placements and future incidents of abuse and may not significantly reduce costs is quite remarkable. Perhaps, more than anything else, it speaks to the desperation among child welfare policymakers, practitioners, and child advocates to find something that works.

The Adoption Assistance and Child Welfare Act of 1980 provides the framework for child welfare policy in the states. The act promoted the goal of permanency in the lives of troubled children by encouraging states to (1) prevent out-of-home placements by keeping families together whenever possible; (2) reunite children with their birth parent or parents as quickly as possible; and (3) encourage adoption for those children who cannot be returned to their family.

Strongly supported by child advocates, child welfare professionals, public interest organizations, professional associations, private foundations, Congress and the Clinton administration, family preservation services are considered to be a key strategy for achieving these objectives and attacking problems confronting the child welfare system (Bond and Rockefeller, 1993, March 3; Subcommittee on Human

Resources, Committee on Ways and Means, 1993, April 29). Moreover, with the enactment of the Family Preservation and Child Protection Reform Act in 1993 and the commitment of $1 billion in federal funds to implement this legislation, family preservation has become virtually the only strategy.

There are many versions of family preservation services. However, notwithstanding diversity, almost all programs have certain elements in common. According to Rossi (1991) these include:

1. *Doctrine of "Risk of Imminent Placement"*: Family Preservation Services are to be given to families with a child "at risk of imminent placement," a determination to be undertaken jointly by the agencies involved. This doctrine implies that there are cases in which placement should [be] made and that there are cases in which neither placement nor FPS is necessary.

2. *Obvious Physical Harm Risk Exclusion*: Placement (instead of services) should be undertaken when there is obvious danger to the physical well-being of the child, any member of the family, or to case workers who might be assigned to the family.

3. *Quick Start*: Services should be started quickly after substantiation and be of limited duration.

4. *Family-Centered*: Services should be directed at all members of a household, not just at either the victim or the alleged perpetrator.

5. *Placement Moratorium*: A moratorium on placement is to be in effect for the duration of the services or until a case worsens to the point that placement is necessary for safety reasons.

6. *High Dosage*: Client families should be provided intensive services with as high a dosage as necessary, often involving visits of several hours duration more than once a week. (Rossi, 1991, p. 23)

Family preservation services are usually delivered for a relatively short period of time--six weeks to two months (Rossi, 1991). In addition, family preservation workers typically have low caseloads, which allows them to be available to families when they are needed (Knitzer and Yelton, 1990; Rossi, 1991).

As mentioned earlier, the popularity of family preservation services can largely be attributed to the promotion and marketing of the services, particularly the "Homebuilders" model, by the Edna McConnell Clark and Annie E. Casey Foundations and because of extraordinary claims of success in preventing out-of-home placements by family preservation advocates (Barthel, 1991; Children's Defense Fund, 1991; U.S. Government Printing Office, 1987, June 9; Schwartz and AuClaire, 1995; Gelles, 1996). For example, Joan Barthel (1991) authored a publication on family preservation services that was funded by the Edna McConnell Clark Foundation. She wrote that "enthusiasm for family preservation is based upon the simple fact it works. It works in cities and in rural farming areas. It works on Indian reservations and in the suburbs" (p. 42). Incredibly, she concluded this while acknowledging "there is not yet proof-using an academically acceptable, experimental design—that family preservation can decrease the number of placements in a state, and therefore save funds that would have otherwise been spent in out-of-home care" (p. 43).

Michigan's "Families First" program is one of the most well known and successfully marketed family preservation programs in the country. Officials from the Michigan Family Independence Agency (FIA) submitted data to the Michigan legislature in 1991 indicating that Families First had a 79.3 percent success rate in preventing out-of-home placements in 2,378 families that were part of a one-year follow-up study (MDSS, not dated). In 1992, John M. Engler, Michigan's governor, delivered a special message on strengthening families, emphasizing that "perhaps the best example of this concept is Families First" (Engler, 1992, p. 19). He claimed the program works and is "a practical alternative to steadily increasing foster care costs and rising caseloads" (p. 22). Susan Kelley, a child welfare bureaucrat who oversees the program in Michigan, testified about the Families First program before the United States Congress and reported that there were declines in the foster care growth rates in counties served by Families First (Kelley, 1990, April 4). Research by others, however, has raised serious questions about whether Kelley's and other similar claims by Michigan FIA officials are accurate (Schwartz and AuClaire, 1995).

A study commissioned by the Michigan FIA indicated that "The Families First Program is effective in preserving families by enabling children to remain with their families, thus averting out-of-home placement." It further concluded that "The Families First Program is highly cost effective when compared to Foster Care Services" (Bergquist, Pope, and Corliss, 1995, p. 3). The researchers estimated the program "may have saved the State of Michigan more than $219,343,000 over the six-year program period" (p. 20).

These are impressive and encouraging findings. Under normal circumstances one would not hesitate to suggest they should be broadly disseminated and used by child welfare policymakers and professionals throughout the country. Unfortunately, because social services have been so highly politicized in Michigan, the findings must be viewed with great caution and skepticism until the study is published in a respected peer-reviewed journal or has been scrutinized by independent and prominent child welfare researchers. In fact, one respected child welfare academic, who wished to remain anonymous, remarked that "the study only has credibility in the state of Michigan!"

A few years ago, Michigan's governor eliminated the state's General Assistance Program. Researchers from the University of Michigan's School of Social Work evaluated the impact of the program and were quite critical of it (*Ongoing*, Summer/Fall 1995, p. 1). The governor, who, at the time, had national political aspirations and was often mentioned as a possible running mate with Bob Dole, appeared on ABC's "Nightline" and dismissed the findings. He claimed he had data from his social services department indicating that the program was a great success. This is an example of just how sensitive and politicized issues related to welfare had become in Michigan.

There are also some other issues that need to be sorted out before any firm conclusions can be drawn from the study. For example, during the time the Families First Program was being implemented there was tremendous pressure coming from FIA's administration to reduce placements and control child welfare costs. Rather than being placed into foster care, a large, but unknown, number of children were placed with relatives (Goerge, Wulczyn, and Harden, 1995, p. 31). In part, this was done to save money because many relative homes were not licensed to accept foster children and, therefore, were not entitled to foster care reimbursement. They may have been eligible for [AFDC] Aid to Families Dependent Children payments, but these subsidies were much less than what they would have received if their homes were licensed for foster care.

The study of the Michigan Families First program may prove to be credible. If it is, it will be an important addition to what is currently known about family preservation services. However, until the study's credibility can be established by reputable and independent sources, it should not be taken too seriously.

Despite the accolades, testimonials, and popularity of family preservation services, serious questions are being raised about their real effectiveness (Littell, Schuerman, and Rzepnicki, 1991; Pecora et al., 1995; Rossi, 1991; Rossi, 1992a; Schuerman, 1992; U.S. Government Printing Office, 1991, March 19; Wald, 1988). As Karger and Stoesz (1997) note, "Two decades of experience with family preservation shows that the blush is off the rose" (p. 3). In the landmark study of family preservation services in Illinois, John Schuerman and his colleagues at the Chapin Hall Center for Children at the University of Chicago concluded that family preservation services had little or no effect on preventing placements or future incidents of abuse (Schuerman, Rzepnicki, and Littell, 1994). In a recent analysis of the data from the Illinois study, Littell (1997) found "that the duration, intensity, and breadth of family preservation services have little impact on subsequent child maltreatment, out-of-home placement, or the closing of cases in child welfare" (p. 34). Littell further concludes that family preservation services cannot be "a remedy for the complex social and psychological problems that contribute to child abuse and neglect, nor is it likely to reduce foster care caseloads. These problems are rooted in poverty, unemployment, inadequate housing, substance abuse, and severe and persistent mental illness" (p. 36).

The most favorable thing that can be said at this time is that "While some preliminary studies of FBS [Family Based Services] are positive, the research findings, particularly those based on more rigorous designs, are mixed" (Pecora et al., 1995, p. 1). Although it may be difficult to accept, the bottom line is that "To date, the field lacks conclusive evidence that FBS prevent child placement and about which types of FBS programs are most effective with different client subpopulations including those involved in physical abuse, neglect, parent-child conflict, delinquency or other areas. We also need a better understanding of effectiveness with different age groups of children and of programs that contribute to success with different families (e.g., in-home services, active listening, client goal setting, concrete services" (Pecora et al., 1995, pp. 8–9). There are problems in implementing the "imminent risk of placement" criterion. It is far too broad and subjective to be meaningful. There are also questions about the appropriateness of using placement prevention as the only criterion for program success (Rossi, 1991; Rossi, 1992a; Rossi, 1992b; Schuerman et al., 1992; Wald, 1988; Pecora et al., 1995).

Mark Courtney, a highly respected child welfare scholar, observes that, "In the absence of empirical evidence of the prevention of family breakup and reduction of child maltreatment in targeted families, continued calls for large-scale family preservation programs will be increasingly hard to justify as anything more than a call for full-employment of social workers" (1997, pp. 74–75). Policymakers, child welfare professionals, and child welfare advocates would be well advised to heed to Courtney's advice.

Some observers are calling attention to the increasing number of children placed out of their homes despite the availability of family preservation services (Whitmire, 1992, March 5). Some are even questioning whether family preservation services will ever achieve large-scale reductions in out-of-home placements (Schuerman et al., 1992; Schuerman et al., 1994). This is a particularly interesting issue because many governors and state legislators were encouraged to support family preservation programs because they were told or led to believe they would reduce the numbers of children being placed into foster care and reduce child welfare system costs.

REFOCUS FAMILY PRESERVATION SERVICES

Although family preservation services have not achieved what their proponents of these services had hoped, at least not to the satisfaction of respected child welfare researchers and informed practitioners, there is some cause for optimism. There is evidence that intensive family-oriented crisis intervention and stabilization services can be effective in preventing placements in costly residential treatment centers, in-patient psychiatric and substance abuse treatment units, and group homes (Schwartz and AuClaire, 1995; Scherer et al., 1994). A substantial and disproportionate amount of child welfare funding is used to pay for emotionally disturbed and troubled children placed in these types of programs. Many, if not most, of these placements can be prevented and treated just as well or even more effectively in other less costly and less intrusive services—for example, home-based crisis intervention services, day treatment, therapeutic foster homes, and a combination of these services (Schwartz, 1994; Schwartz and Beker, 1994).

The vast majority of family preservation programs are targeted to prevent the placement of abused and neglected children in family foster care. Instead of keeping the focus on preventing placements in foster care, which may cost $30 a day or less per child, child welfare administrators would be well advised to use their family preservation resources on preventing placements in the more expensive programs and where the evidence suggests they can be more cost effective.

With the enactment of the Adoption and Safe Families Act of 1997, Congress committed itself to spending more than $1 billion on family preservation and support programs over the next four years. This commitment continues the federal funding support that started with the Family Preservation and Support Act of 1993. While we have no illusions about how difficult it would be to redeploy these resources, we nonetheless strongly recommend that state and local elected public officials and child welfare administrators do just that. More specifically, they should redeploy some of their family preservation services resources toward preventing costly residential care placements and in reducing the lengths of stay in these facilities. Table 2-1 lists the estimated allotments to states and other jurisdictions for family preservation and support programs authorized under the Adoption and Safe Families Act of 1997.

Table 2-1
Adoption and Safe Families Act of 1997 State and National Allotments
FY's 1998 - 2001 (dollars in thousands)

State	FY 1998 Estimate	FY 1999 Estimate	FY 2000 Estimate	FY 2001 Estimate
Alabama	4,567	4,952	5,283	5,462
Alaska	366	395	395	438
Arizona	4,384	4,728	5,072	5,244
Arkansas	2,238	2,414	2,589	2,677
California	31,719	34,207	36,695	37,938
Colorado	2,398	2,586	2,774	2,868
Connecticut	1,918	2,068	2,219	2,294
Delaware	479	517	554	573
District of Columbia	799	862	924	965
Florida	12,423	13,397	14,372	14,859
Georgia	6,691	7,216	7,741	8,003
Hawaii	822	886	951	983
Idaho	662	714	766	792
Illinois	9,226	9,950	10,673	11,035
Indiana	4,133	4,457	4,781	4,943
Iowa	1,598	1,723	1,849	1,911
Kansas	1,484	1,600	1,717	1,775
Kentucky	3,928	4,236	4,544	4,698
Louisiana	6,851	7,388	7,926	8,194
Maine	982	1,059	1,136	1,175
Maryland	3,219	3,471	3,724	3,850
Massachusetts	3,859	4,162	4,464	4,616
Michigan	8,495	9,161	9,828	10,161
Minnesota	2,764	2,981	3,198	3,306
Mississippi	4,270	4,605	4,940	5,107
Missouri	4,749	5,121	5,494	5,680
Montana	548	591	634	655
Nebraska	982	1,059	1,136	1,175
Nevada	799	862	924	956
New Hampshire	457	493	529	547
New Jersey	4,475	4,826	5,177	5,352
New Mexico	2,055	2,216	2,377	2,458
New York	16,190	17,460	18,730	19,365
North Carolina	5,115	5,516	5,917	6,118
North Dakota	366	395	423	438
Ohio	10,094	10,886	11,677	12,037
Oklahoma	2,923	3,152	3,382	3,496
Oregon	2,170	2,340	2,510	2,595
Pennsylvania	9,020	9,727	10,435	10,789
Rhode Island	799	862	924	956
South Carolina	3,311	3,571	3,830	3,960
South Dakota	457	493	529	547
Tennessee	5,617	6,058	6,498	6,718

Texas	22,493	24,257	26,021	26,903
Utah	1,165	1,256	1,348	1,393
Vermont	457	493	529	547
Virginia	4,179	4,507	4,835	4,998
Washington	3,700	3,990	4,280	4,425
West Virginia	2,649	2,857	3,065	3,168
Wisconsin	3,014	3,250	3,487	3,605
Wyoming	296	319	342	354
Other	6,271	6,763	7,255	7,501
Total	**234,626**	**253,028**	**271,421**	**280,639**

Source: Fiscal Planning Services, Inc., Bethesda, MD

There is certainly no credible evidence that the federal as well as the state funds already spent on such family preservation programs are having much of an impact on preventing the propulsion of children into foster care, and the prognosis for the future is, at best, guarded. Neither is there credible evidence that these funds are providing enhanced protection for abused and vulnerable children. Therefore, governors, state legislators, child welfare administrators, and child advocates would be well advised to redeploy their family preservation services funds to areas in which they can do the most good. It would be unfortunate if this opportunity were lost and these resources squandered because it is unlikely that we will see a large infusion of new federal funds in children's services for a very long time.

Some people in the child welfare field maintain that family preservation services should be provided whether they prevent placements or not. They argue that they fill an important supportive function for troubled families. This may be the case. However, this perspective must be weighed against other options and priorities. When this is done, the ill-defined family supportive perspective with a lack of clear outcomes pales in significance compared to the potential for curbing and, possibly significantly reducing, expenditures and placements in congregate care residential and institutional settings.

WHY FAMILY PRESERVATION SERVICES "DIDN'T DO THE TRICK?"

Family preservation services are certainly well meaning. The child advocates and child welfare professionals who support these services are dedicated and committed individuals. They want to be advocates for what they believe to be in the best interests of troubled families. They believe, as do most Americans, in the value of the family; and, to the extent possible, they want to do whatever they can to strengthen families and their ability to stay together and cope with their environments and the stresses they face.

However, as well intentioned as these values and beliefs may be, they underestimate or ignore the social and economic context in which these families live. As was noted in chapter 1, the reality is that the overwhelming majority of families who are the primary source of referrals to the child welfare system are deeply adversely affected by economic depravation. Again, as was noted, a booming economy does not seem to be able to help them economically. In addition, many of these families are heavily impacted by drugs, crime and criminality, and deteriorating living conditions in urban neighborhoods.

In light of this, it is understandable why Senator Moynihan and other students of child welfare reforms and the condition of families in America were skeptical about the potential impact of a progressive sounding, but limited, intervention like family preservation. Any attempt to change the behavior of families that does not really address the underlying and fundamental causes that make these families so weak in the first place is doomed to failure. Also, as Besharov and Laumann (1997) noted, "Society should acknowledge the overlap between child maltreatment and poverty—and adopt intervention strategies that address the families' broader problems" (p. 5). Perhaps if family preservation services were delivered as part of a much broader and more comprehensive social and economic strategy to combat poverty and other related problems confronting inner-city neighborhoods they might have more of a positive impact. As an isolated program, coupled with the fact that we know very little about which families might be amenable to such an intervention, they have had little value and are unlikely to make a significant difference in the future.

REFERENCES

Adoption Assistance and Child Welfare Act of 1980, 42 U.S.C. p. 670.

Barthel, J. (1991). *The promise of family preservation*. New York: Edna McConnell Clark Foundation.

Bergquist, C.; Pope, G.; and Corliss, K. (1995). *Evaluation of Michigan's families first program summary report*. Lansing, MI: University Associates.

Besharov, D. J. and Laumann, L. A. (1997). Don't call it child abuse if it's really poverty. *Journal of Children and Poverty, 3*(1), 5–36.

Bond, C.S., and Rockefeller, J.D., IV. (1993, March 3). *Family preservation and child protection reform* (CPR). Correspondence to U.S. Senators. Washington,DC.

Children's Defense Fund. (1991). *S.4, The Child Welfare and Preventive Services Act*. Washington, DC: Author.

Courtney, M. E. (1997). *Review of Putting Families First. Children and Youth Services Review,* 19, 61–76

Davis, M.; Yelton, S.; Katz-Leavy, J.; and Lourie, I. S. (1995). Unclaimed children revisited: The status of state children's mental health service systems. *Journal of Mental Health Administration, 22*(2), 147–66.

Engler, J.M. (1992). *To strengthen Michigan families*. Lansing, MI: Department of Social Services.

Gelles, R. J. (1996). *The book of David*. New York: Basic Books.

Goerge, R. M.; Wulczyn, F. H.; and Harden, A. W. (1995). *An update from the multistate foster care data archive: Foster care dynamics 1983–1993*. Chicago: The Chapin Hall Center for Children at the University of Chicago.

Karger, H .J., and Stoesz, D. (1997). Learning from family preservation. *Children and Youth Services Review,* 19, 1–4.

Knitzer, J. E. (1981). Child welfare: The role of federal policies. *Journal of Clinical Child Psychology, 10*(1), 3–7.

Knitzer, J. (1982). Children's rights in the family and society: Dilemmas and realities.

American Journal of Orthopsychiatry, 52(3), 481–95.

Knitzer, J., and Yelton, S. (1990). Collaborations between child welfare and mental health. *Public Welfare, 48*(2), 24–46.

Littell, J. H. (1997). Effects of duration, intensity, and breadth of services. *Children and Youth Services Review,* 19, 17–39.

McLarin, K. J. (1995). Slaying of Connecticut infant shifts policy on child abuse. *New York Times,* p. A1.

Moynihan, D. P. (1996). *Miles to go: A personal history of social policy.* Cambridge, MA: Harvard University Press.

National Commission on Children. (1991). *Beyond rhetoric: A new American agenda for children and families.* (Final report). Washington, DC: United States Government Printing Office.

North American Council on Adoptable Children (NACAC). (1990). *The adoption assistance and child welfare act of 1980 (Public law 96–171): The first ten years.* St. Paul, MN: Author.

Ongoing. (Summer/Fall 1995). Ann Arbor, MI: The University of Michigan School of Social Work.

Pecora, P. J.; Fraser, M. W.; Nelson, K. E.; McCroskey, J.; and Meezan, W. (1995). *Evaluating family-based services.* New York: Aldine de Gruyter.

Rossi, P. H. (1991). *Evaluating family preservation programs: A report to the Edna McConnell Clark Foundation.* Amherst: University of Massachusetts.

Rossi, P. H. (1992a). Assessing family preservation programs. *Children and Youth Services Review, 14,* 77–97.

Rossi, P. H. (1992b). Some critical comments on current evaluations of programs for the amelioration of persistent poverty. *Focus, 14* (1), 22–24.

Scherer, D. G.; Brondino, M. J.; Henggeler, S. W.; and Melton, G. B. (1994). Multisystemic family preservation therapy: Preliminary findings from a study of rural and minority serious adolescent offenders. Special series: Center for mental health services research projects. *Journal of Emotional & Behavioral Disorders, 2*(4), 198–206.

Schuerman, J. R.; Rzepnicki, T. L.; and Littell, J. H.; and Associates. (1991). *Evaluation of the Illinois family first placement prevention programs: Progress report.* Chicago: Chapin Hall Center for Children at the University of Chicago.

Schuerman, J. R.; Rzepnicki, T. L.; Littell, J. H.; and Budde, S. (1992). Implementation issues. *Children and Youth Services Review,* 14, 193–206.

Schuerman, J. R.; Rzepnicki, T. L.; and Littell, J. H. (1994). *Putting families first.* New York: Aldine de Gruyter.

Schwartz, I. M. (1994). Child caring institutions: The "Edsels" of children's services. In E. Gambrill and T. Stein (Eds.), *Controversial issues in social work.* Boston: Allyn and Bacon.

Schwartz, I. M., and AuClaire, P. (Eds.). (1995). *Home-based services for troubled children.* Lincoln: University of Nebraska Press.

Schwartz, I. M.; and Beker, J. (1994). Does institutional care do more harm than good? In E. Gambrill and T. J. Stein (Eds.), *Controversial issues in child welfare* (pp. 275–89). Boston: Allyn and Bacon.

Schwartz, I.; Ortega, R.; Guo, S.; and Fishman, G. (1994). Infants in nonpermanent placement. *Social Service Review, 68*(3), 405–16.

U.S. Government Accounting Office. (1993, April 29). *Foster care: Services to prevent out-of-home placements are limited by funding barriers.* Washington, DC: U.S. Government Printing Office.

U.S. Government Printing Office. (1987, June 9). *Home based services for troubled children.* Hearings before the Subcommittee on Ways and Means, House of Representatives. Washington, DC: Author.

U.S. Government Printing Office. (1991, March 19). *State of the nation's child welfare system* (Serial 102–3). Hearings before the Subcommittee on Ways and Means, House of Representatives. Washington, DC: Author.

Wald, M. S. (1988). Family preservation: Are we moving too fast? *Public Welfare, 46*(3), 33–46.

Whitmire, R. (1992, March 5). State spending on child services varies widely. Washington, DC: Gannett News Service.

Wulczyn, F., and Goerge, R. M. (1992). Foster care in New York and Illinois: The challenge of rapid change. *Social Service Review, 66*(2), 278–92.

CHAPTER 3

The Adoption Assistance and Child Welfare Act: Good Intentions Gone Awry

The Adoption Assistance and Child Welfare Act of 1980 is the foundation for contemporary child welfare policy in the United States. The act requires states to make "reasonable efforts" to prevent the removal of children from their homes. If children have to be taken away from their parents, the act encourages that they be returned as quickly as possible and when it is safe to do so. The legislation also mandates that individualized treatment plans be developed for each child placed into foster care and that theses places be reviewed at least once every six months to insure that children receive the care and treatment they need so that permanent plans can be made for them (e.g., return home, adoption, or placement with relatives). The act strongly encourages states to develop family preservation programs (see chapter 2) as a primary strategy for preventing out-of-home placements and for keeping families intact (P.L. 96-272).

The act has enjoyed strong bipartisan support at the national level. Conservatives and liberals embraced it. Conservatives liked it because they thought it supported the family and traditional "family values." They also believed it might save money or, at least, help control escalating child welfare costs. The mushrooming costs of foster care and residential treatment were troubling to fiscal conservatives in Congress. Liberals liked the act because family preservation services held out the promise of keeping families together and preventing unnecessary placements in an overburdened, entrenched, and, frequently, abusive child welfare system. They also thought the act would be a vehicle for reforming the child welfare system in the United States.

WAS THE ACT SUCCESSFUL?

The Adoption Assistance and Child Welfare Act has not been systematically and objectively evaluated. However, although the act has escaped close scrutiny, it is fair to say that the professional child welfare establishment, child advocates and child advocacy organizations, private foundations, the Clinton administration, and most members of Congress have supported the act and believe it has been successful.

Nevertheless, the act has its critics, and their voices are beginning to be heard (Gelles, 1996; MacDonald, 1994; Schuerman, Rzepnicki, and Littell, 1994). There is also data that raises serious questions about its overall effectiveness. For example, as stated earlier, one of the major goals of the act was to reduce the number of children in foster care. This was to be accomplished by preventing unnecessary placements in the first place and by reunifying children who were placed into foster care with their birth parent(s) or legal guardians as quickly as possible. The data in Table 3-1 indicates that there was a modest decline in the foster care population rate between 1980 and 1983. However, the rate increased in 1984 and skyrocketed between 1985 and 1990.

Table 3-1
Children in Foster Care in the United States 1962-1994

Year	U.S. Foster Care[1]	U.S. Population Ages 0-18[2]	Rate (per 1,000)
1962	272,000	69,864,000	3.89
1963	276,000	71,164,000	3.88
1964	287,000	72,406,000	3.96
1965	300,000	73,520,000	4.08
1966	309,400	73,179,000	4.23
1967	309,600	73,429,000	4.22
1968	316,200	73,396,000	4.31
1969	320,000	74,000,000	4.32
1970	330,400	73,516,000	4.49
1971	319,800	73,665,000	4.34
1972	N/A	72,369,000	N/A
1973	N/A	72,243,000	N/A
1974	N/A	72,070,000	N/A
1975	N/A	71,402,000	N/A
1976	N/A	70,500,000	N/A
1977	N/A	69,699,000	N/A
1978	N/A	67,003,000	N/A
1979	N/A	68,307,000	N/A
1980	302,000 [3]	67,913,000	4.45
1981	274,000 [3]	67,571,000	4.05
1982	262,000 [3]	67,118,000	3.90
1983	269,000 [3]	66,768,000	4.03
1984	276,000 [3]	66,863,000	4.13
1985	276,000 [3]	66,797,000	4.13
1986	280,000 [3]	66,932,000	4.18
1987	300,000 [3]	67,221,000	4.46
1988	340,000 [3]	67,709,000	5.02
1989	383,000 [3]	67,877,000	5.64
1990	407,000 [3]	67,246,000	6.05
1991	429,000 [3]	68,527,000	6.26
1992	442,000 [3]	69,470,000	6.36
1993	445,000 [3]	70,411000	6.32
1994	469,073 [3]	71,367,000	6.32

[1] Data from Child Welfare Research Notes #8 (July 1984), published by Administration for Children, Youth and Families, HDS, HHS.

[2] U.S. Census Bureau, Population Division, unpublished data (1962-1994); U.S. Department of Commerce, Bureau of the Census, Statistical Abstract for the United States, 1985, 1990.

[3] Data were collected using a variety of methodologies and may not be comparable with each other or with other years.

Supporters of the act refer to the decline in the number and rate of children placed into foster care in the early 1980s as evidence of the legislation's success. They usually attribute the subsequent increase in the foster care population to cutbacks in federal domestic spending during the Reagan administration and to the drug problem, particularly the crack epidemic that burst onto the scene in the mid-1980s. The modest decline in the rates between 1980 and 1983 can hardly be called a success story, particularly in light of the enormous increase in federal appropriations for the federal Foster Care and Adoptions Assistance Programs since its inception (see Figure 3-1). Also despite the leveling off in federal obligations between 1996 and 1998, they are estimated to increase significantly in fiscal year 1999.

Figure 3-1
Federal Foster Care Appropriations and Obligations
Fiscal Year 1982–1999

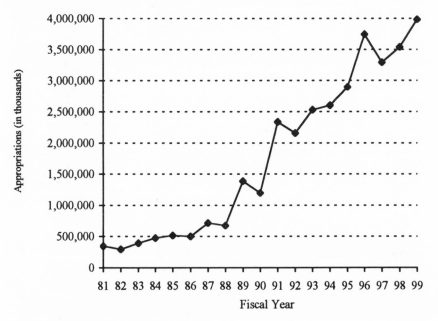

Source: Fiscal Planning Services, Inc., Bethesda, MD.
Note: Includes federal Title IV-E funds only.
           Does not include state and local foster care dollars.
           Figure for 1999 is estimated.

In addition, there are serious questions about the comprehensiveness, reliability, and comparability of the available national child welfare data reported by the federal government during the early years. In fact, the federal government cautions people to be leery about the reliability of the data and how it can be used (see note 3, in table 3-1). This, of course, raises questions about whether the decline in the number of children in foster care during the early 1980s was as great as it appears or more of an artifact resulting from the changes in the way the data was collected.

The act's supporters also maintain that the number of children in foster care would have been much higher if the legislation had not been enacted. While this may be plausible, there is no hard supporting evidence. Frankly, we have doubts that this would have been the case. Nevertheless, this is an argument that is often made.

The cutbacks in federal domestic spending have eroded the social safety net in the United States (Gelles, 1996). This, coupled with the crack epidemic, undoubtedly contributed to the dramatic increase in the child welfare population (MacDonald, 1994; Gelles, 1996). These are forces, however, that the act was not designed or expected to address. Neither was the act designed to address poverty, another key factor considered important for preventing child welfare placements (Gelles, 1996; Lindsey, 1994; Pelton, 1992).

REASONABLE EFFORTS

The architects of the Adoption Assistance and Child Welfare Act and those who lobbied successfully for its enactment were particularly proud of the fact that the legislation included the "reasonable efforts" concept. They felt this was a major victory and would be an important mechanism for preventing hasty removal of children from their homes. They believed it would force child protection workers to systematically explore all reasonable options and resources that should be considered to prevent out-of-home placements and that they would be held accountable for doing so by juvenile and family courts. They also thought it would lead to the creation of alternative services and resources in jurisdictions where they simply didn't exist or were in short supply. "Despite the law's good intentions, it planted seeds of trouble. The goal of child protection services became safeguarding children while also working to reunite them with their abusive parents. The assumption was that these mandates could be balanced successfully. The reality was that the demands were contradictory" (Gelles, 1996, p. 94).

This dilemma was compounded by the fact that the authors of the act failed to define "reasonable efforts." This has led to confusion about how to implement the intent of the legislation (Gelles, 1996; Edna McConnell Clark Foundation, no date; North American Council on Adoptable Children, August 1990; Seaberg, 1986). For example, the act mandates that "in each case, reasonable efforts will be made (A) prior to the placement of a child in foster care, to prevent or eliminate the need for removal of the child from home, and (B) to make it possible for the child to return to his home" (P. L. 96–272, sec. 471 a. 15, p. 503).

Unfortunately, "Nowhere in the federal legislation, state policy, or ensuing legal decisions in state courts were 'reasonable efforts' ever clearly defined. As a result, child protection workers, administrators, and legal staff had no guidelines for how much or how long they had to make 'efforts' at reunification before moving to permanent placements for abused and neglected children" (Gelles, 1996, p. 94). Such diverse groups as the National Council of Juvenile and Family Court Judges, the Child Welfare League of America, the Youth Law Center, and the National Center for Youth Law worked together to try to define and clarify the concept of "reasonable efforts" (Edna McConnell Clark Foundation, no date). Unfortunately, their work fell far short of the mark. Not surprisingly, this led to enormous disparities in child protection policies and practices throughout the country.

Some argue that failing to define this concept has resulted in children being left in dangerous and life-threatening situations (Gelles, 1996). For example, Connie Binsfeld, Michigan's lieutenant governor, delivered some powerful and compelling testimony about reasonable efforts before the U.S. House Ways and Means Subcommittee on Human Resources on June 27, 1996. She told the subcommittee members that

Today, "reasonable efforts" have become "unreasonable efforts" as we provide services again and again to abusive parents. Children are entering foster care more damaged because they are left in their abusive homes while workers attempt to prove the unprovable to the federal government-that the undefined nebulous "reasonable efforts" have been made to prevent the removal of the children from their home. Because children are more damaged upon entering the system, our foster care and adoption subsidy costs have soared due to intensive care these children need. Their damage is compounded as they are shuffled from disrupted placement to disrupted placement due to their behavior and overwhelming needs. They become unadoptable.

We need to challenge the present trend of our child welfare system, which is based on the "reasonable efforts" provision that implies that every family can be "fixed" and a biological family, regardless of the severity of its dysfunction, is always the best place to raise a child.

Binsfeld astutely noted that "The rights of the adults override the needs of the child. In my opinion, reuniting a child with an abusive parent is nothing less than ordering a beaten wife to return to live with her abusive husband. The abused wife is no longer seen as the property of her husband. It is time we free our children from similar bondage." These are perspectives with which we totally agree.

In addition, as we pointed out in chapter 2, the act strongly encouraged child welfare agencies to develop services to prevent out-of-home placements. This legislation was subsequently reinforced when Congress enacted the Family Preservation and Child Protection Reform Act and committed itself to pumping $1 billion in federal funds over a five-year period into family support and family preservation services (Senate, S.596). Family preservation programs were already under serious attack because they were ill conceived and oversold. As we and others have noted, they lacked a sound theoretical and practical foundation that is based upon any known credible research. This is a problem that still exists today (Gelles, 1996). More importantly, family preservation programs are being questioned because they are used indiscriminately, which often results in children being kept in harm's way.

Barth and his colleagues have noted that the increase in the foster care population resulted from steadily increasing growth in entries into care as compared to exits (Barth et al., 1994). Moreover, the gap between entries and exits has widened, particularly after FY 86 (VCIS report, August, 1993). This accounts for the large increases in the foster care population in the latter half of the 1980s. The years 1991 and 1992 show a narrowing of that gap, but the difference is still quite pronounced and still far higher than what it was in the first part of the 1980s.

Nationally, many children enter the foster care system due to an emergency referral (Lindsey, 1992). However, according to Lindsey (1992), the decision to take a child away from his or her biological parents is often determined by income adequacy. There is also evidence to indicate that incidences of abuse, particularly physical abuse, are more likely to be referred for in-home services while neglect cases tend to be referred for out-of-home placement (Saunders, Nelson, and Landsman, 1993). One may logically hypothesize that neglect is more closely associated with poverty than abuse. Some corroboration for this hypothesis is found in the fact that since World War II, African American children have been overrepresented in out-of-home care (Saunders, Nelson, and Landsman, 1993). Currently, over 40 percent of the children in the welfare system are African American (an estimated 200,000 out of 460,000). This should not be surprising since African Americans, particularly African American children, are disproportionately impacted by poverty in the United States.

PERMANENCY AND REUNIFICATION

Once children are placed into foster care, the Adoption Assistance and Child Welfare Act (P.L. 96–272) places a premium on reunifying them with their biological parents. If that is not possible, then the Act encourages that other permanent plans (e.g., adoption or placement with relatives) be developed and carried out. The act requires formal reviews of each foster child's case at least once every six months (Green Book, 1993). This is required in order to insure accountability and to monitor services delivered to children being cared for by the government. If a child cannot be returned home within eighteen months, the act mandates that other permanent plans be implemented at time (P.L. 96-272).

A number of studies have looked for factors that contribute to successful family reunification and the prevention of recidivism or reentry into foster care (Block, 1981, November; Fein and Staff, 1993, January; Goerge, 1990, September; Lawder, Povlin, and Andrews, 1986; U.S. General Accounting Office, 1991; Wulczyn, 1991; Wulczyn and Goerge, 1992). Early research showed that once a child is in care for more than eighteen months the probability for returning home is greatly diminished (Maas and Engler, 1959; Goerge, 1990, September). This early pioneering research was the major driving force behind the six and eighteen month case review and permanency planning requirements built into the Act. Subsequent research showed the eighteen month figure was inflated due to a "length bias" from an overrepresentation of children in care for a very long time (Goerge, 1990, September, p. 425).

This later research also indicates that case reviews should begin within weeks of a child's initial out-of-home placement, and should be routinely conducted at relatively short intervals thereafter; further, that permanency options other than returning a child home can and should be developed much earlier than eighteen months (Goerge, 1990, September, p. 449). Despite these important later findings, the old policies requiring case reviews at least once every six months and an eighteen month time limit for developing and implementing alternative permanency plans were in effect until the enactment of the Adoption and Safe Families Act of 1997. Also, although the act requires formal case reviews once every six months, rarely are such reviews conducted before that time. In other words, reviewing cases at six months has become the norm.

Although there have been some studies on the topic of reunification, many questions about this issue remain unanswered. Many of the questions about reunification cannot be answered because of the poor state of national child welfare data. For example, very limited and reliable national data is available on the number of children in substitute care, the duration of their care, precisely where they go when they leave care, and whether they are returned to care (Tatara, 1993). Accurate and reliable data on how many children are actually reunited with one or both of their biological parents is simply not available. In some states, placing children with relatives, particularly grandparents, is considered "family reunification" and counted as if they were placements with biological parents. In Michigan, placement with relatives is not even considered to be an out-of-home placement, at least this was the case when we conducted our research. This gives a very skewed picture about how the child welfare system in that state really functions, what really happens to children who come to the attention of child welfare authorities, and the results of programs designed to prevent placements and to reunify foster children with their biological parents. Also, kinship placements in Michigan are not routinely paid as if they were foster parents unless they apply and meet the appropriate standards. Needless to say, this provides a significant economic incentive for placing foster children with relatives.

Our limited understanding about reunification is made even more complicated by the fact that, on occasion, official agencies and organizations misinterpret data on this subject. For example, the National Commission on Children (1991) noted:

The stated goal of every child in foster care is reunification with his or her natural parents or placement in an adoptive home. It is commonly believed that with about two-thirds of the children, that goal is ultimately met. For instance, the National Commission on Children reported that in 1986 slightly fewer than 60 percent of the children in foster care were either reunited with their families or placed with a parent, relative, or other caregiver (National Commission on Children, p. 288). Courtney, as recently as 1997, claims that "Studies since the 1960s have shown that around two-thirds of children placed in out-of-home care are eventually returned to their families of origin, most after relatively short stays in care" (p. 68).

As encouraging and widely accepted as these figures are, there is reason to believe they may be inaccurate and misleading. According to Tatara (1993), the correct interpretation is: "nearly two-thirds of children (58.8 percent in FY 86, 63.0 percent in FY 89) *who left substitute care* were either reunified with their families or placed with a parent, relative, or caretaker" (p. 73). In other words, of those children exiting substitute care, approximately two-thirds were reunified. As stated earlier, there are serious questions about how many children actually exit the child welfare system, at least within a reasonable period of time. There are just as many questions about how many of these children are placed back into the child welfare system at a later date. A sizable but unknown number of children do not exit the system until they "age out" (reach legal adulthood). Also, many are placed into the system and end up staying in it for years before they exit. This is particularly the case for infants and other young children. For example, researchers at the Chapin Hall Center for Children at the University of Chicago found that infants in the foster care systems in Michigan, California, New York, Illinois, and Texas stay significantly longer (at least 20 percent longer) in out-of-home placement than do children in other age groups (Goerge, Wulczyn, and Harden, 1994). Wulczyn (1994) found that in New York City "infants typically remain in foster care longer than older children" (p. 169). He also noted "that fewer infants leave their first placement within ninety days, and more infants remain in care for two or more years" (p. 169). Barth and his colleagues have been carefully studying the child welfare system in California for a number of years. They concluded that "overall, it appears that slightly less than one half of the children entering foster care (in California) for the first time will be reunified with their parents within three years" (Barth et al., 1994, p. 113). This data is particularly important as 70 percent of those children that will eventually be reunified go home within the first year. The percentage drops off significantly after that, with the chances for reunification after three years being slim (Barth et al., 1994).

The data we examined from Michigan's Children's Services Management Information System suggest that, contrary to conventional wisdom, perhaps less than one-third of the children removed from their homes due to abuse or neglect in that state may be successfully reunified with one or both of their biological parents within four years. As striking as this may be, it might not be as unusual as some may think. In an analysis of national child welfare data Tatara (1994) found

that the proportion of children exiting the substitute care system became continually smaller in recent years, highlighting the fact that the number of substitute care exits has not kept pace with the growing number of children in care. In programmatic terms, this finding is very important to the public child welfare community because it suggests that there has been a decline in the child welfare system's effectiveness in helping achieve permanency of care for substitute care children. The recent decline in substitute care exit rates is a troubling sign that children are no longer leaving substitute care at the same rates as they were in the early 1980s. (p .136)

The data from California, Michigan, and now from the rest of the country raise a number of important questions. For example:

1. Can the number of children placed into foster care who are *successfully* reunified with

one or more of their biological parents be significantly increased, and, if so, what would it take to accomplish this?

2. Are the relatively low rates of reunification in California and Michigan and the declining overall national rates a reflection of informed and reasonable professional judgments by child welfare workers or are there other factors that account for these developments?

3. What are the experiences with respect to reunification in other states?

4. What were the assumptions about reunification at the time the Adoption Assistance and Child Welfare Act was passed? Were those assumptions valid then, and are they still valid today?

The professional child welfare community and researchers in the field obviously have a responsibility to look into these issues before new solutions are proposed or large scale investments are made to try to improve existing programs. However, elected public officials and other policy makers need to do some introspection as well. In particular, they must take a hard and careful look into whether the policies they embraced and the resources they allocated to address the problem of reunification and permanency were appropriate. For example, we and others suspect that the families from which the bulk of the child welfare caseload is coming are so severely damaged and afflicted with such "deeply rooted societal problems (e.g., poverty, joblessness, inadequate housing, poor education), which are far beyond the ability of any one social welfare program alone to solve" (Tatara, 1994, p. 142). These fundamental problems are the real issues that must be addressed, and the child welfare system, no matter how well intentioned the policies and well funded the system may be, is clearly incapable of tackling these issues by itself (Tatara, 1994).

Relatives have always played a role in caring for children of their kin. The difference between this long standing tradition and growing contemporary practice is that previously, such care did not involve the state. The policy in many states is to pay relatives for care at the same rate as other foster parents. In Illinois, for example, between 1981 and 1992 the proportion of children in relative care increased from 24 percent to 53 percent of all children in foster care (Schuerman, Rzepnicki, and Littell, 1994). According to Wulczyn and Goerge (1992), other states are experiencing the same trend. Placements with kin are often perceived as preferable by child welfare professionals when out-of-home placement is inevitable. Child welfare administrators and social workers think of kinship care as upholding the principles of the least restrictive alternative and of permanency. The homes of relatives are sometimes viewed by the child welfare workers as almost the same as a child's natural home—if not better, as the risk of harm to the child is smaller and extended family ties are maintained. Two goals that are not achieved by placing children in foster care with relatives are reunification with birth parents and reducing or controlling child welfare expenditures. "As research shows, children in kinship foster care are reunified at very slow rates" (Barth et al., 1994, p. 261). As a result, the costs for kinship placements are higher than for traditional foster care because the length of stay in homes with relatives tends to be considerably longer (Schuerman, Rzepnicki, and Littell, 1994; Barth et al., 1994). Another concern about kinship placements is the possibility that the abusing or neglectful parent(s) may continue to be in the picture and have contact with the children even though this may not be desirable or should only be allowed under close supervision.

Family preservation services are considered to be one of the major resources in helping children achieve permanency. "Family preservation aims to decrease the number of children placed in foster care by quickly teaching their abusing or neglectful parents the skills necessary to keep the family together" (MacDonald, 1994, p. 45). These services can also be deployed to reunite families after children have been removed from their homes. Some of the more strident advocates of family preservation services believe that almost any of the problems families face can be corrected with the right "mix" of therapy and social services. The premise is that abusive parents are victims themselves, and their behavior toward children is a consequence of circumstances and environment and not part of the character of the abuser. Unfortunately, as we and others have noted, there is no credible scientific evidence that family preservation programs result in substantial reductions in out-of-home placements or that they prevent future incidences of abuse or neglect. There is also no satisfactory and reliable method for identifying those families who might be amenable to such interventions (Gelles, 1996; Schuerman, Rzepnicki, and Littell, 1994). This means that absent such tools, children have been, and continue to be, left in harm's way under the progressive sounding, but substantively bankrupt, policy rhetoric of family preservation. There is also scant evidence that family preservation services are effective in reuniting families either.

Another source for achieving permanency is adoption. Adoption, while an attractive and viable option, is, in reality, the "stepchild" of permanency planning alternatives. It does not receive the priority consideration it should, and, as a result, it has been grossly underutilized. For example, as we have noted, the number of foster care children who are adopted each year through public agencies is amazingly low. In fact, only about 22,500 of the more than 500,000 children reported to be in foster care at the end of fiscal year 1996 in the United States were adopted, with an additional 7,000 being permanently placed in legal guardianships (Craig and Herbert, 1997). Sadly, another 53,642 who were eligible for adoption were not adopted. This track record has led Barth and colleagues to conclude that, "At this time, adoption does not provide a major exit from foster care for America's children" (Barth et al., 1994, p. 263).

President Clinton has called for doubling the number of adoptions and permanent legal guardianships to 54,000 by the year 2002. Even if the president's goal is reached, it represents only a modest gain in the permanency issue. In other words, adoption will still not be a major vehicle for exiting the child welfare system. The question that must be asked is: Why are so few children being adopted when so many of them, particularly infants and toddlers, are kept in foster care for years or reenter foster care because their parents cannot take care of them?

RE-ENTRY INTO FOSTER CARE

Unfortunately, because of all the rhetoric and policy emphasis on family preservation, permanency, and reunification, relatively little attention has been paid to the important topic of reentry into foster care. When it has been studied, some of the inquiries have been sloppy. For example, the U.S. General Accounting Office (GAO) in September 1991 issued a report on child welfare in which reentry into foster care was one of the issues examined. The GAO looked at children who were unsuccessfully reunified and determined that those who were kept out-of-home initially for at least a year had a better chance of being successfully reunified with their families. In their report to the U.S. Senate Finance Committee, the GAO noted: "These results suggest that minimizing [the] length of stay may not always be in the best interest of the child" (U.S. General Accounting Office, 1991, p. 5).

The problem with this analysis is that the GAO only considered those children who were returned home. As we mentioned earlier, Barth's research in California and our data from Michigan show that many children are never returned home (at least within any reasonable period of time) and that the longer they are in substitute care the more their chances for reunification decrease. For most children, the GAO's policy recommendation would be harmful.

One study of foster care reentry after children were reunited with their families in California does begins to shed some light on this issue (Courtney, 1995). The researchers found the children reentering the foster care system to be relatively young and about equally divided by gender. One third were under four years of age when they exited care and one half were under seven. Older children (seven to twelve year olds) had a much better chance to "make it" once they exited the foster care system than did infants and other young (one to four year olds) children. The researchers also found that race and poverty have a major impact on foster care reentry. For example, the probability for African-American children from AFDC-eligible families reentering the system is twice that of Caucasian families not eligible for AFDC. The study also revealed that the first few months following discharge are the most critical. The researchers noted that while foster care reentry rates by themselves are not a good measure of permanence for children, family reunification rates cannot be meaningfully judged independently of reentry rates.

PERMANENCY AND REUNIFICATION IN MICHIGAN

The findings from our research into Michigan's child welfare system are remarkably similar to the findings of others and to the national trends reported in this chapter. Overall, this means that many of the children in Michigan's child welfare system over the last decade did not benefit from the hopes and dreams embodied in the Adoption Assistance and Child Welfare Act. For example, from the sample of 77,444 children we examined in Michigan's (CSMIS) data set, over half had no record of ever having been returned home within four years after their initial placement. One-third did not have a record indicating they had any permanent placement within that time.

In our analysis of the living arrangements of the children, we discovered there were a small number of children (8.5 percent of the total sample) who were kept at home even though child welfare workers recommended them for out-of-home placement. Although the reasons why these children were never placed are unclear, there are a number of plausible explanations. For example, the crisis which led to the decision to remove the children may have dissipated before foster care workers removed them, and then the workers subsequently decided removal was not necessary. This finding, although curious, is not unique in Michigan (Schwartz and AuClaire, 1995; Schuerman, Rzepnicki, and Littell, 1994). In any case, we are confident that the overwhelming majority of children we studied from the CSMIS data set were removed from their homes.

One of the most disturbing findings was that almost 66 percent of the children who started out by being removed from their homes and placed into Michigan's foster care system had no record of ever (at least within four years) having been successfully returned home, (see Figure 3-1) More alarming was the fact that 85 percent of these children had no record in their files of ever having been returned to their biological families, even for a short period of time. Also, 9.6 percent were returned home at least once but ended up back in the system. The children who were initially removed from their homes had only a 28 percent chance of returning home successfully. Considering that the system is supposed to make reunification and family preservation a priority, these are poor results. They are generally consistent, however, with the findings reported by others (Barth et al., 1994; Schuerman, Rzepnicki, and Littell, 1994). Interestingly, the records revealed that the small number of children who were referred to foster care but were not initially removed from their homes had an 81 percent chance of remaining at home or of ending up back with their families if they were subsequently placed into the system.

Clearly, where a child starts, either at home or in substitute care, is a critical predictor of where a child will end up. The very first decision about whether a child can remain at home can determine his or her career in the child welfare system. Some of the other factors that seem to have an effect on reunification, at least in Michigan, are discussed below.

Age

The data suggests that the probability of returning home varies with the age of children entering the system. Keeping in mind that the chances of successfully returning home in general are only slightly more than one in four (or 28 percent), we found that children who enter the system between the ages of five and ten appear to have a much better chance for reunification than is the case with infants, toddlers, preteenagers, and teenagers. In fact, infants and adolescents had the lowest chances of all. The low probability of reunification for adolescents is not surprising and has been noted by others (Fein and Maluccio, 1992). The poor chance for infants of being reunified with their families is a more recent phenomenon (Wulczyn and Goerge, 1992).

Length of Stay in Placement

Given that where a child starts (whether they start at home or not) is an important predictor, we would expect length of stay in placement(s) also to be important. And, indeed it is. The longer a child remains in his or her first placement, the lower the probability for achieving permanency. The chances for achieving permanency during the first few months in placement exceed the probability for remaining in out-of-home care. However, after approximately six months, the probability of achieving permanency is less than the probability for remaining in foster care. After one year, children in Michigan's foster care system have less than a 40 percent chance of ever achieving permanency. Similar to the findings of others (Goerge, 1990), the longer a child remains out-of-home in Michigan, the less likely he or she is to be returned home. However, we also found that the relatively small proportion of children who were returned home tended to stay there.

These findings raise a number of important issues that need to be examined further. For example, the emphasis in Michigan and in many other states on family preservation and reunification borders on being an obsession (Gelles, 1996). It is as if families must be reunified and preserved almost to the exclusion of other options. Perhaps the overemphasis on trying to reunify children with their parents should be abandoned and replaced with a strategy that is more child centered, more realistic, and takes more and quicker advantage of other permanency options (e.g., adoptions, placement with relatives, and long-term foster care). The relatively low probability for reunification for those initially removed from their homes may not necessarily be bad but might well be an indication that the level of dysfunction that exists in families is such that these parents are not capable of caring for their children even after parents and children have been separated for an extended period of time.

Race

The historical inequities in the delivery of child welfare services for African American children are well known (Fein and Maluccio, 1992; Pinderhughes, 1991; Gelles, 1996). Approximately 17 percent (U.S. Bureau of the Census, 1990) of Michigan residents under the age of eighteen are African American; however 41 percent of the children in the CSMIS data set are African American. National data estimate the percentage of African Americans in substitute care to be 34 percent (Tatara, 1993, p. 92).

For African American children and other children of color (e.g., Hispanics and Native Americans), where they start is even more important. For those who remain at home and are part of that small group of children who are recommended for placement but are never actually placed, their chances of remaining home are fairly good. However, for African American children who start out-of-home, their chances of returning home is lower (23 percent) than is the case for Caucasian children (30 percent). Children in the "other" category have the worst chance of returning home. Without better information about who these children are, it is difficult to know why this is the case. This is another example of the need for better data, particularly data on how child welfare outcomes differ by race.

Despite having a lower chance for reunification, African American children appear to have about the same chance of achieving permanency as do Caucasian children. This might be due to the fact that African American children are often placed with relatives. For example, we found that 38 percent of African American children had been placed with a relative at some time during their child welfare careers, in comparison to only 29 percent for Caucasian children. Moreover, the CSMIS records indicated that 20 percent of African American children and 13 percent of Caucasian children were *only* (i.e., permanently placed) with a relative.

Like virtually all large data sets, the CSMIS data includes a category of children defined as "Other." This includes Hispanics, Native Americans, and those of other and unknown races or ethnicities. Such children had a lower probability of achieving permanency than did either the Caucasian or African American children.

Long-Term Foster Care

The CSMIS records indicated that almost one-third of the children in Michigan's foster care systems were *never* placed in a potentially permanent living arrangement. Many of these children are in long-term foster care, which is definitely not one of the options emphasized in P.L. 96–272 (Barth and Berry, 1987). Many states appear to use long-term foster care as a permanent placement. For example, data from twenty-nine states in FY 89 showed that 11.9 percent of the children had a goal of long-term foster care (Tatara, 1993).

At the time we conducted our research, the long-term foster care policy in Michigan was somewhat unclear. According to the foster care services manual, workers should help children return home or move to an appropriate permanent placement as soon as possible. However, the manual also says that "After a child has been with a family 12 months or more, that family is to be considered the psychological family" (MDSS, 1991, November 8, p. 8). The manual goes on to say that "the child shall not be removed solely for the purpose of achieving a 'more successful' placement," and "a placement is considered permanent if it is intended to last indefinitely" (MDSS, 1991, November 8, p. 2)

The decision to leave a child in long-term foster care raises a number of issues that need to be carefully examined by policy makers and professionals. To begin with, there probably are some children who need some kind of long-term substitute care because they cannot be reunified with their parents or placed with relatives, and are unlikely to be adopted. If this is the case, then policy makers and professionals must recognize this fact and plan accordingly. Our hope is that many, if not most, of the parents of these children would have their parental rights terminated and that child welfare authorities would be aggressive in trying to have these children adopted. After all, there is evidence that the special needs adoptions movement appeared to have a significant impact in the 1970s and 1980s.

Richard Gelles, in his thoughtful *The Book of David*, suggests that "orphanages like Boys Town in Nebraska or the Milton Hershey School in Pennsylvania" might be an appropriate option for these children (Gelles, 1996,

p. 163). We are not quite as confident as Gelles about the merits of long-term group or congregate care living arrangements for abused and neglected children. We would have to see some hard and compelling evidence about this approach before we could support it. Accordingly, we believe that policymakers and professionals would be well advised to find permanent family homes for these children and should be certain that this and other alternatives have been fully exhausted before considering institutional living arrangements. Also, if there is a need for some foster families to provide long-term care rather than temporary care, they should be recruited with that purpose in mind and provided with adequate long-term support and resources. With such support, long-term foster care could be a reasonable and viable alternative when reunification or adoption is not possible (Fein and Maluccio, 1992).

Given the successful "permanence" of these nonpermanent placements, we wonder whether it might not be possible for more of these children to become better candidates for reunification, placement with relatives, legal guardianship, or adoption. If not, then policy makers and professionals will have to face the fact that a large proportion of children placed into substitute care will essentially be the permanent responsibility of the government. This reality also has serious implications that need to be carefully examined because long-term foster care was never envisioned to be an option for achieving permanency.

REFERENCES

Barth, R. P., and Berry, M. (1987). Outcomes of child welfare services under permanency planning. *Social Service Review, 61*(1), 71–90.

Barth, R. P.; Courtney, M.; Berrick, J. D.; and Albert, V. (1994). *From child abuse to permanency planning*. New York: Aldine de Gruyter.

Block, N. (1981, November). Toward reducing recidivism. *Child Welfare, 60*(9), 597–610.

Courtney, M. (1995). Re-entry to foster-care of children returned to their families. *Social Service Review, 69*, 226–41.

Craig, Donna, and Herbert, D. (1997). *The state of the children: An examination of government-run foster care*. National Center for Policy Analysis.

Edna McConnell Clark Foundation. (No date). *Making reasonable efforts: Steps for keeping families together*. New York: Author.

Fein, E., and Maluccio, A. N. (1992). Permanency planning: Another remedy in jeopardy. *Social Service Review, 66*(3), 335–48.

Fein, E., and Staff, I. (1993, January). Last best chance: Findings from a reunification services program. *Child Welfare, 72*(1), 25–37.

Gelles, R. J. (1996). *The book of David*. New York: Basic Books.

Goerge, R. M. (1990, September). The reunification process in substitute care. *Social Service Review, 64*(3), 422–57.

Goerge, R. M.; Wulczyn, F. H.; and Harden, A. (1994). *Foster care dynamics 1983–1992: A report from the multistate foster care data archive*. Chicago: The Chapin Hall Center for Children, University of Chicago.

Green Book. (1993). Implementation and effects of foster care reforms. *Background material and data on major programs within the jurisdiction of the Committee on Ways and Means*. Washington, DC: U.S. Government Printing Office.

Lawder, E. A.; Povlin, J. E.; and Andrews, R. G. (1986). A study of 185 foster children 5 years after placement. *Child Welfare, 65*(3), 241–51.

Lindsey, D. (1992). Reliability of the foster care placement decision: A review. *Research on Social Work Practice, 2*(1), 65–80.

Lindsey, D. (1994a). Mandated reporting and child abuse fatalities: Requirements for a system to protect children. *Social Work Research, 18*(1), 41–54.

Lindsey, D. (1994b). *The welfare of children.* New York: Oxford University Press.

Lindsey, D., and Trocme, N. (1994). Have child protection efforts reduced child homicides? An examination of data from Britain and North America. *British Journal of Social Work, 24*(6), 715–32.

Maas, H. S., and Engler, R. E., Jr. (1959). *Children in need of parents.* New York: Columbia University Press.

MacDonald, H. (1994). The ideology of family preservation. *Public Interest, 115,* 45–60.

Michigan Department of Social Services (MDSS). (1991, November 8). *Children and youth services manual.* Lansing: Author.

Michigan Kids Count. (1992). *1992 data book.* Lansing: Michigan League for Human Services.

National Commission on Children. (1991). *Beyond rhetoric: A new American agenda for children and families.* (Final Report). Washington, DC: U.S. Government Printing Office.

North American Council on Adoptable Children (NACAC). (1990, August). The Adoption Assistance and Child Welfare Act of 1980 (Public Law 96-171). *The first ten years.* St. Paul, MN: Author.

Pelton, L. H. (1989). For reasons of poverty: *A critical analysis of the public child welfare system in the United States.* New York: Praeger.

Pelton, L. H. (1991). Beyond permanency planning: Restructuring the public child welfare system. *Social Work, 36*(4), 337–43.

Pelton, L. H. (1992). A functional approach to reorganizing family and child welfare interventions. *Children and Youth Services Review, 14*(3–4), 289–303.

Pinderhughes, E. E. (1991). The delivery of child welfare services to African American clients. *Orthopsychiatry, 61*(4), 599–605.

Rzepnicki, T. L. (1987). Recidivism of foster children returned to their own homes: A review and new directions for research. *Social Service Review, 61*(1), 56–70.

Saunders, E. J., Nelson, K., and Landsman, M. J. (1993). Racial inequality and child neglect: Findings in a metropolitan area. *Child Welfare, 72*(4), 341–54.

Schuerman, J. R., Rzepnicki, T. L., and Littell, J. H. (1994). *Putting families first.* New York: Aldine de Gruyter.

Schwartz, I. M. and AuClaire, P. (1995). *Home-based services for troubled children.* Lincoln: University of Nebraska Press.

Schwartz, I. M., Ortega R. M., Guo, S., and Fishman, G. (1994). Infants in non-permanent placement. *Social Service Review, 68*(3), 405–16.

Seaberg, J. R. (1986). "Reasonable efforts": Toward implementation in permanency planning. *Child Welfare, 65*(5), 469–79.

Spar, K. (1993, March 24). *Child welfare and foster care: Issues in the 103rd Congress.* Washington, DC: Congressional Research Service.

Tatara, T. (1990). *Children of substance abusing and alcoholic parents in public child welfare.* Washington, DC: American Public Welfare Association.

Tatara, T. (1993). *Characteristics of children in substitute and adoptive care.* Washington, DC: American Public Welfare Association.

Tatara, T. (1994). The recent rise in the U.S. child substitute care population: An analysis of national child substitute care flow data. In R. Barth, J. Durer Berrick, and N. Gilbert (Eds.), *Child Welfare Research Review*, pp. 126–45.

U.S. Bureau of the Census. (1990). Current population reports. (Series P-25). Washington, DC: U.S. Government Printing Office.

U.S. General Accounting Office (GAO). (1991). *Foster care: Children's experiences linked to various factors; Better data needed.* Washington, DC: U.S. Government Printing Office.

Wulczyn, F. (1991). Caseload dynamics and foster care reentry. *Social Service Review*, *65*(1), 133–56.

Wulczyn, F. (1994). Status at birth and infant placement in New York City. In R. Barth, J. Durer Berrick, and N. Gilbert (Eds.), *Child Welfare Research Review*, pp. 146–84.

Wulczyn, F., and Goerge, R. M. (1992). Foster care in New York and Illinois: The challenge of rapid change. *Social Service Review*, *66*(2), 278–92.

CHAPTER 4

Adopted: Who Is and Who Isn't?

National data on adoptions suffers from the same deficiencies as does all other child welfare data. It is incomplete, not particularly reliable, and doesn't allow for meaningful interjurisdictional comparisons. Available statewide data is sparse to nonexistent in many states. This makes it virtually impossible to formulate a clear national and state-by-state perspective on adoption trends and issues (Tatara, 1993; Finch, Fanschel, and Grundy, 1991; Flango, 1990). For example, a recent Child Welfare League of America (CWLA) publication, *Child Abuse and Neglect: A Look at the States* (1997), included data on the number of children who were adopted from public child welfare agencies in 1993. Data from the public agencies in forty-seven states showed that 27,115 children were legally adopted during 1995 (Petit and Curtis, 1997, p. 124). In the same document, it is reported that 125,248 children were adopted from various and supposedly all known public and private sources in 1992. It is estimated that approximately 40 percent were adopted from public agencies, which would bring the number of public agency adoptions to 50,000 (Petit and Curtis, 1997). More recently, President Clinton was quoted as indicating that the number of public agency adoptions was approximately 20,000 in 1995 and that his goal for the country was to get to "at least 54,000 children adopted or permanently placed from the public foster care system by 2002" (The White House Office of the Press Secretary, 1997, November 4).

It is sad to observe that we are in the midst of an information and technological revolution and yet we are incapable of getting an accurate picture on how many children are adopted in the United States and from what sources. Among other things, this severely limits the ability of policymakers and professionals really to understand the dimensions of the phenomenon they are dealing with and to develop meaningful and rational policies and solutions.

As stated above, the Child Welfare League of America reported that 125,248 children were adopted from all public and private sources in 1992. According to the league, this figure was up from the 118,216 children adopted in 1987. Although this may appear to be encouraging to some, in reality, it amounts to no increase at all because the rate per thousand adopted in 1987 was 1.9 and was the same in 1992. This is sobering and raises serious questions about the prospects for President Clinton's hope to double the number of children to be adopted from just public sources.

The information presented in this chapter provides some interesting insights into adoption policies and practices in Michigan. It is a microscopic look into Michigan's system. While the findings cannot be generalized to the rest of the country, they are generally consistent with the findings of other research into such states as California and New York. The Michigan findings also highlight some important issues and questions that need to be examined more carefully.

Among the growing number of children removed from their homes and placed into substitute care, the majority is assumed to be there temporarily. Not surprisingly, the increase in the number of children removed from their homes has been accompanied by a steady growth in the number of children who are legally and permanently separated from their parents (Tatara, 1993). This means that more children are eligible for adoption. In 1987, for example, 118,216 children were adopted from public child welfare agencies and/or their private agency conduits. By 1992, the number had increased to 125,248.

While the increase was encouraging, most child welfare experts acknowledge that the number of children who should be adopted each year could be much greater. Although only twenty-two states responded, a 1994 CWLA survey on adoptions revealed that out of the total number of children for whom adoption was set as a goal, only 30 percent were legally free for adoption. Moreover, over the past decade, adoption has been the permanency plan for only 14 percent of all children placed into substitute care (Tatara, 1993, p. 134).

"Between FY 83 and FY 89, more children with special needs were adopted than those who had no known special needs" (Tartara, 1993, p. 134). However, the growth in adoptions of children with special needs has been accompanied by a corresponding increase in adoption disruptions. Although not entirely due to complexities in adopting children with special needs, minimizing adoption disruptions is one of the major challenges facing adoption services today (Barth et al., 1988; Hairston and Williams, 1989; McDonald et al., 1993; Rodriguez and Meyer, 1990; Rosenthal, Groze, and Curiel, 1990).

There are other major challenges confronting adoption services. For example, child advocates and reformers maintain that the child welfare bureaucracy creates impediments to adoption (Hearing before the Subcommittee on Human Resources, 1991). Older children have always had difficulty being adopted. Sadly, because of their age, they are often viewed as "damaged goods" (i.e., they may have long histories of abuse and/or neglect as well as serious emotional and behavioral problems; and they may have been further damaged while in the custody of the child welfare system); thus, they are not particularly attractive to prospective adoptive parents. Infants, one of the fastest growing age groups in child welfare (Wulczyn and Goerge, 1992), have about the same prospects for achieving permanency, including adoption, as adolescents (see chap. 3).

THE MICHIGAN EXPERIENCE

In Michigan, as in most states, adoption is a complex mixture of laws, regulations, guidelines, and professional opinion. Most children eligible for adoption represent cases where parental rights are terminated involuntarily. Many of these children have been neglected and/or abused, and adoption may occur only after the child resides in substitute care for several years.

Michigan relies heavily on private adoption agencies, accounting for over half of all adoption placements. According to the Michigan Adoption Factbook (1991), private adoption efforts in Michigan focus primarily on infants, children with special needs, and international children.

At a minimum, screening criteria for adoption require that the following are present: motivation for adoption, parenting ability, emotional stability, and compatibility between the adoptee and adopting parent(s). The following may also influence a successful adoption outcome: adoptive family members' attitudes toward accepting an adoptive child, criminal convictions of the adoptive parent(s), and characteristics of the adoptive parents that will best serve the needs of the adoptee. As can be seen, some of these criteria are quite subjective.

ADOPTION TRENDS IN MICHIGAN

Michigan's CSMIS data set includes case closure information and allows three adoption outcomes to be distinguished: placement, confirmation, and disruption. There are some indications that CSMIS may not reflect all adoption activity occurring within the state. For example, CSMIS maintains adoption records separately from substitute care records. When a child moves from a nonadoptive placement into adoption placement, the case is assigned a new identification number even though it may pertain to the same child. While this assures confidentiality for adopted children, it is difficult to connect child welfare preadoption with postadoption careers for these children. We have also learned that case closing information is not always reliable and requires a considerable amount of "cleaning" before analysis. We found, for example, a few instances where the closing code was nonsensical (e.g., an infant case closed due to marriage), inconsistent, or incomplete.

Despite these quirks and limitations, CSMIS data can be used to shed some light on the past decade's adoption trends and stimulate the examination of important and basic questions: Who is placed for adoption? Who achieves adoption? Who adopts? Who does not achieve adoption? Do subsidies make a difference in adoption practices?

Table 4-1 presents information about two subpopulations of all child welfare youth with case closing information: adoption placement and not placed for adoption. Children without close code information were not included. In addition, a child was not included if the case was closed due to death, marriage, military enlistment, or leaving the state. *Adoption placement* was defined as those cases in which probate court (the juvenile court) issued an order to place a child for adoption with Michigan Family Independence Agency supervision. Parental rights were terminated in these cases. *Not placed for adoption* is defined as those cases that were closed for reasons other than adoption, such as placement into a permanent living arrangement, aging out of the child welfare system, reunification with family, and juvenile justice outcomes (e.g., completion of probation).

The table reflects the percent distributions of children placed and not placed for adoption between 1982 and 1991 by race, age, and disability status. Among the adoption placement population, these distributions indicate that over the decade in question, Caucasians, infants as well as children between the ages of three and ten years, and nonhandicapped children were most likely to exit the child welfare system to an adoption placement. African Americans accounted for 31 percent of the children placed for adoption, while Hispanics and other children of color accounted for 4-1 percent of adoption placements. Children between the ages of one and two years made up 10.4 percent of adoption placements while children eleven years and older accounted for only 10.5 percent of these placements. Finally, of the children with an impairment or disability who were placed (15.3 percent of the total population), those classified as having a psychological impairment accounted for 8.2 percent of the placements while children with physical or sensorial disability (e.g., hearing and visually impaired) made up 7.1 percent of the placement population.

Table 4-1 indicates a lower percent distribution of Caucasian children among the not-placed population, compared to their distribution among adoption placements. On the other hand, African American children have a higher percent distribution among not-placed children compared to their distribution among adoption placements. The percent distributions for Hispanics and other children of color are relatively similar when comparing those placed and not placed for adoption.

Table 4-1
Michigan Child Welfare Comparison of Percent Distribution
of Children Placed and Not Placed for Adoption 1982–1991

	Total Youth N=(44,971)	Placed for Adoption (7,956)	Deviation from Population Distribution	Not Placed for Adoption (37,015)	Deviation from Population Distribution
Race					
Caucasian	56.3	64.9	.15	54.4	-.03
African American	39.7	31.0	-.22	41.6	.05
Hispanic	1.8	1.7	-.09	1.9	.02
Other	2.2	2.4	.11	2.1	-.02
Age					
Infants (0-1)	13.9	29.9	1.16	10.4	-.25
1 - 2	7.1	10.4	.47	6.4	-.10
3 - 5	17.1	23.6	.37	15.8	-.08
6 - 10	21.6	25.6	.18	20.8	-.04
11 -15	25.9	9.7	-.62	29.3	.13
15+	14.3	0.8	-.95	17.3	.20
Handicaps					
Psychological	5.9	8.2	.41	5.3	-.09
Physical	2.4	5.7	1.40	1.7	-.30
Sensoral	0.6	1.4	1.37	0.4	-.29
None	91.2	84.6	-.07	92.6	.02

Source: Michigan Department of Social Services CSMIS data analyzed by the Center for the Study of Youth Policy.

Notes: 0 indicates perfect distribution.
"Deviation from population distribution" = (a/b) - 1 where a = category and b = total population inclusive of category a.

The percent distribution for placed and not placed also reveals two particularly pronounced variations according to age. Whereas infants made up 29.9 percent of the adoption placement population, they only account for 10.4 percent of the population not placed for adoption. The implication is that infants faired better over the decade in their representation among cases closed to adoption placement than nonadoption placements. On the other end of the age spectrum, children age eleven years and older accounted for 10.5 percent of the children placed for adoption and 46.6 percent of the children not placed for adoption. Here, the implication is the opposite of that of infants: beginning around preadolescence, the likelihood of older children exiting the system as a nonadoptive placement is much higher than as an adoptive placement. The fact that infants are likely to be placed for adoption is not surprising. Once termination of parental rights occurs, one would expect a goal of adoption for them. The decline in adoption placements observed in table 4-1 as children become older is consistent with previous reports in the literature. As it appears now, adoption for children past the age of ten is less likely because a smaller percentage are being placed for adoption. It certainly underscores the need to explore the special needs of older children to facilitate their adoption placement or else to identify alternative permanency arrangements.

Among children with disabilities, 7.4 percent of the children with a designated disability who exited child welfare did not achieve an adoptive placement. Compared to those placed for adoption (15.3 percent), this distribution reflects a greater likelihood among disabled children of exiting child welfare as an adoptive placement rather than as a nonadoptive placement. This is not surprising given the major emphasis over the past decade to place special needs children (in this case, children with disabilities). If the goal in adoption policy was to increase the placement of these children, the data suggest that this is being achieved with relative success. On the other hand, the goal of adoption placement of children of color appears less impressive over the past decade. These children will undoubtedly benefit from increased attention.

Issues regarding children who do and do not achieve adoption can be explored through examining adoption confirmation and adoption disruption outcomes. For *adoption confirmation* cases, probate court has issued a final order confirming the adoption petition and dismissed court wardship. In *adoption disruption* cases, probate court has issued an order to dismiss an adoption petition prior to confirmation of the adoption.

Table 4-2 presents information about confirmations and disruptions between 1982 and 1991 by race, age, and disability status. As this table indicates, 19 percent of case closing data included in the study population (between 1982 and 1991) were confirmed adoptions. This refers to over 9,000 cases equally distributed among males and females. Less than 1 percent of the case closings (.8 percent) were due to adoption disruption. This is below what has been reported in other studies (from 1.5 percent to over 20 percent), although there is no national figure available for comparison (North American Council on Adoptable Children, 1991). Part of the problem is that some studies include disruptions among both preadoption and postadoption confirmation cases, while others use either preconfirmation or postconfirmation cases. In the present study, only pre-adoption confirmation disruptions are considered.

Table 4-2
Michigan Child Welfare Comparison of Percent Distribution
of Children in Confirmed and Disrupted Adoptions 1982–1991

	Total Youth N=(46,433)	Adoption Confirmed (9,006)	Deviation from Population Distribution	Adoption Distribution (412)	Deviation from Population Distribution
Race					
Caucasian	55.0	57.2	.04	66.7	.21
African American	40.0	33.9	-.15	26.7	-.33
Hispanic	1.8	1.2	-.33	1.7	-.06
Other	3.2	7.7	1.41	4.9	.53
Age					
Infants (0-1)	9.4	5.6	-.40	--	--
1 - 2	6.7	8.2	.22	2.2	-.67
3 - 5	18.1	27.6	.52	14.6	-.19
6 - 10	23.6	34.6	.47	33.5	.42
11 -15	27.5	19.9	-.28	42.5	.55
15+	14.7	4.1	-.72	2.3	-.84
Handicaps					
Psychological	6.8	12.3	.81	22.3	2.28
Physical	2.7	6.9	1.56	6.3	1.33
Sensoral	0.6	1.5	1.50	1.7	1.88
None	89.8	79.4	-.12	70.0	-.22

Source: Michigan Department of Social Services CSMIS data analyzed by the Center for the Study of Youth Policy

Notes: 0 indicates perfect distribution.
"Deviation from population distribution" = (a/b) - 1 where a = category and b = total population inclusive of category a.

Among confirmed adoptions, table 4-2 indicates that roughly 57 percent were Caucasian; 34 percent, African American; and 8 percent, other children of color. Hispanics made up the smallest percentage of children among adoption confirmations over the decade (1.2 percent). In terms of age, children between the ages of three and ten years accounted for 62.2 percent of confirmed adoptions. An additional 19.9 percent of adoption confirmations were among children between eleven and fifteen years of age. Only 13.8 percent of confirmed adoptions occurred for children under two years of age. Adoption confirmations over the decade included 20.7 percent of children with disabilities.

Table 4-2 also presents the percent distribution of disrupted adoptions recorded over the past decade. In total, only a small proportion of the adoption population resulted in disruption (.8 percent). Caucasians made up 66.7 percent of these disruptions, followed by African Americans (26.7 percent). In terms of age, 76 percent of disruptions occurred among children between the ages of six and fifteen years. Another 14.6 percent of disruptions occurred for children between three and five years of age, and only 2.2 percent of adoption disruptions occurred for children under two years of age. Finally, 30 percent of the disrupted adoptions occurred among children with disabilities. The majority of these disruptions occurred among psychologically impaired children (22.3 percent).

Table 4-3 utilizes predicted probabilities based on a logistic regression model to examine important characteristics of children placed for adoption. In general, when all case closings are considered, the results indicate that children entering the child welfare system have a .11 probability of being placed for adoption. In terms of age, infants are most likely, of all age groups, to be placed for adoption (.39). The probabilities for adoption placement steadily decline although somewhat dramatically after the age of ten years. There were no differences in the probability of adoption placement by gender. The probability of adoption was highest for Caucasians (.14) and lowest for African Americans (.08). Regarding placement relative to disability status, the results indicate a higher probability of adoption for impaired or disabled children (.27) compared to nondisabled children (.10). Finally, in the interest of examining whether or not there was a cohort effect, the results indicate a slightly higher probability of adoption placement in the period from 1982 to 1985 (.12) as compared to the period from 1986 to 1991 (.11).

These results confirm, in a more statistically rigorous way, what was discovered using observations of the percent distributions. However, they do illuminate in a way unparalleled by other studies the chance of being placed, and therefore being available for adoption, according to important factors such as age, race or ethnicity, and disability. Clearly, these results point to the need for further exploration in an effort to find out why these patterns emerged, particularly since there were noticeable differences in actual adoptions, as observed in table 4-2.

Table 4-3
Predicated Probability of Being Placed for Adoption 1982-1991

All	.11

Age of Entry	
Infant	.39
1	.27
2-9	.22
10-11	.10
12-13	.05
14-15	.02
16+	.01
Gender	
male	.11
female	.11
Race	
Caucasian	.14
African American	.08
Hispanic	.11
other	.12
Disability	
yes	.27
no	.10
1982-1985	.12
1986-1991	.11

Note: Number in study, 44,971.

In summarizing table 4-2, the distributions suggest that those children most likely to achieve adoption confirmation entered the child welfare adoption system between the ages of three and ten years. One can only speculate about why this would be the case. It may suggest that the adoption process is best suited for noninfant preschool children and those well into elementary school, and it pinpoints the ages of children preferred by adoptive parents. A major inconsistency is the fact that a number of infants will be placed for adoption, as indicated in table 4-1, but will not achieve adoption confirmation. This raises further questions about the adoption process for infants.

Keeping in mind that the number of disruptions is much smaller than the number of confirmations in Michigan, the pattern that emerges shows that children between the ages of eleven and fifteen years were more likely to experience adoption disruption and less likely to experience confirmation. It is commonly understood that adolescents have multiple negative experiences prior to and during their child welfare careers and are therefore difficult cases for any type of permanency planning. While the literature points to this difficulty among adolescents, the results of this study suggest that in practice adoption difficulties probably begin earlier, with preadolescents.

The likelihood of being adopted is also greater for Caucasian and children of other ethnic groups (e.g., Native Americans and those of other and unknown races or ethnicities) and for ages six to ten among handicapped children. However, among disruptions these children also appear in disproportionately higher numbers. The results suggest that, when comparing percent distributions, adoption success (confirmed adoption) should not lose sight of adoption failure (adoption disruption). This relationship speaks to the importance of applying what is known about the successes of the adoption process to prevent adoption failures.

To nobody's surprise, our data reveals that over the past decade two parents were more likely to adopt than a single parent. However, there appears to be a convergence between these family types so that single parent adoptions have gained in prominence (see figure 4-1).

Figure 4-1
Michigan Child Welfare System Youth Confirmed for Adoption
Comparison of Adopting Family Type—Single and Two Parent
1982-1990

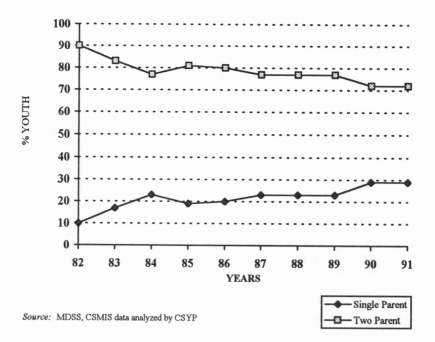

Source: MDSS, CSMIS data analyzed by CSYP

Trends over the period 1982 to 1990 also point to a reversal of prominence among relatives, nonfoster parents, and foster parents. Figure 4-2 indicates that a larger portion of adoptions occurred among nonfoster parents in the early 1980s, although foster parent adoptions essentially replaced this more traditional adoptive family type during the mid-1980s. This in some ways supports speculation about the rise in the number of foster parents achieving adoption. The trend for foster parents to adopt raises some interesting dilemmas: Can foster parents who want to adopt really help in trying to reunify children with their birth parents? To what extent can they help place children with relatives? What about the potential for a conflict of interest? To what extent can the shortage of foster homes be attributed to the increase in foster parent adoptions?

Figure 4-2
Michigan Child Welfare System Youth Confirmed for Adoption
Comparison of Adopting Family Type—Foster, Non-Foster and
Relative 1982-1990

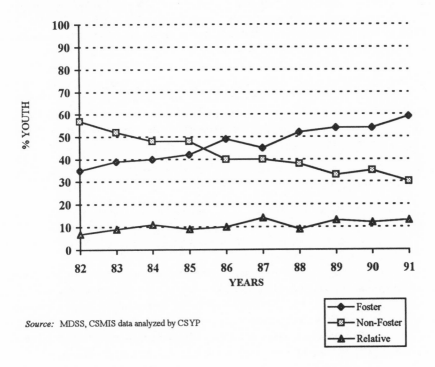

Source: MDSS, CSMIS data analyzed by CSYP

Adoption by relatives, although a small proportion of all adoptions (about 11 percent), also appeared to be gaining in prominence toward the late 1980s. It would be interesting to know what the circumstances are which prompt adoption by relatives.

Adoption subsidy has been perceived to be very instrumental in facilitating adoptions, but that might not be the case. The majority of confirmed adoptions occurring during the 1980s in Michigan were associated with an adoption subsidy, and most were tied to medical and nonmedical types of support. In 1982 roughly 50 percent of adoption confirmations occurred with a medical and/or a nonmedical subsidy, and in 1991 this increased to nearly 88 percent. Perhaps the real question is, Did the number of adoptions increase? In other words, did the increase in subsidized adoptions also increase the number of adoption confirmations?

In 1982, there were 945 confirmations recorded in CSMIS as compared to 1,065 recorded in 1991. This reflects a 13 percent increase in the number of adoptions between these two years. In other words, despite a substantial increase in the percent of adoptions with a subsidy, there was only a modest increase in the number of adoptions during the period. One could assume that the original intent of providing subsidies was both to support the number or children available for adoption and to increase the number of adoptions. There was some evidence of this plan working after 1985, although a net increase in the number of adoption confirmations was not apparent until after 1989. Ideally, such incentives could help to improve the quality of life for these children and their adoptive families and even minimize the number of disruptions. It is not clear why these incentives were relatively ineffective in achieving both their intended goals, particularly in increasing the number of adoptions until 1989.

POLICY IMPLICATIONS

The Michigan data reveals that the adoption process does not work equally well for all children. This, of course, is not surprising. What is surprising is that some of the common assumptions about who is adopted and who is not do not seem to apply.

For example, the finding that infants are not well represented among confirmed adoptions needs closer scrutiny. In general, the knowledge we have gained about infants in Michigan's child welfare system runs counter to conventional wisdom. In chapter 3, we pointed out that over half of all infants placed out of their homes will not achieve a permanent home within four years of their initial placement. They are being raised by the state without H.O.P.E. (home or other permanent environment—the home of a relative, legal guardian, an adoptive home, or an independent living arrangement).

One could argue that infants simply cannot achieve adoption confirmation until they are at least age one because of the time it takes to terminate parental rights and be placed for adoption. The data in table 4-2 runs counter to this argument, as the vast majority of adoption confirmations occur for children ages two years and older.

As we pointed out in chapter 3, we are also troubled by the fact that one-third of all children initially placed out of their homes never achieve H.O.P.E. Of this population, 25 percent are infants. The good news is that the overwhelming majority of children who never achieve H.O.P.E. have had only one placement. However, these children are essentially "adopted" by the state and are "confirmed" to permanent foster care. While these foster homes provide a stable environment, and the children in them are probably psychologically attached to their foster parents, we wonder about the potential for these children to be adopted, or, at the very least, to achieve the federal goal of permanency. We wonder what is known about these children when they are first placed and at what point does it become apparent that they are without H.O.P.E. and will have to be raised by the state. We also wonder whether family preservation and reunification policies, which currently are so predominant, are creating a mind-set of an undying hope that children in placement will and must be returned to their natural parent or parents at all costs, even when this is not a realistic possibility and may even be dangerous. Although not widely discussed in child welfare circles, perhaps the goal of permanent foster care will have to be acknowledged as a fact of life for a large proportion of children who are removed from their natural parents?

Also, at least in these cases, the concept of family reunification may have to be reconsidered possibly as a range of contact and relationship possibilities with birth parents. (Maluccio, Fein, and Davis, 1994; Maluccio, Warsh and Pine, 1993; Courtney, 1993). Individuals who are eighteen and over have a variety of types of relationships and interactions with their families. It isn't simply all or nothing. Some people can only have a satisfactory relationship with their parents if they see them periodically. Some can live with their parents and some cannot. Some may not be able to see their parents at all and can only have a relationship by telephone or correspondence. Why, then, should we expect anything different for people under the age of eighteen? Family reunification does not, and should not, have to mean an actual return to the natural family in order to be considered a success.

We are particularly perplexed and troubled by the fact that such a large proportion of these children are infants when there are so many people wanting to adopt children of this age. Prospective adoptive parents are usually told there are no infants available to adopt, and that they will have to be put on a long waiting list. They become frustrated and often adopt an infant from another country at considerable financial and personal cost.

Clearly, impediments to confirming adoptions must receive priority attention. This is not a particularly a novel idea and we are certainly not alone in recognizing the necessity and urgency for this (Hewlett and West, 1998). Although the majority of children in permanent foster care are not bouncing around from placement to placement, it is unacceptable for so many of them, particularly infants, essentially to grow up in foster care when the goal is to apply permanent placement options.

We also think child welfare administrators, child advocates, adoption advocates and policymakers in other states would be well advised to examine this issue to see if it is a problem in their child welfare systems. Based upon our findings in Michigan, we would not be surprised if large numbers of children are being raised in permanent foster care situations by other states. We would also not be surprised to find a large number of these children began as infants.

It is generally understood that older children are least likely of all age groups to be adopted. We found that children age eleven and older are considerably underrepresented in placement for adoption and in having adoptions confirmed. In addition, although there are relatively few disrupted adoptions, children aged eleven to fifteen years were highly represented in this category. Interestingly, this was not the case for children over fifteen years. This latter finding runs counter to the belief that the oldest children carry with them a history of problems putting them at high risk of adoption disruption.

The fact that preadolescent children as young as age eleven are not well represented among adoption placements and confirmations is disconcerting. This may, in part, be accounted for by the fact that these children are more likely to achieve permanency in other ways as compared to other age groups. However, it also raises the possibility that children age eleven years and older may be perceived as "damaged goods" and undesirable for adoption. If true, this is a cruel perception and one needing immediate and careful consideration by policymakers and practitioners. This issue needs to be examined by researchers, child advocates, and child welfare professionals in other jurisdictions.

As stated earlier, strategies encouraging the adoption of children with special needs were emphasized during the 1970s and 1980s. There has been so much progress in this area in Michigan that children with disabilities are more likely to be adopted than are children without disabilities. We must continue to make progress with respect to adopting disabled children, but we should also take steps to insure that other children are not left behind. In addition, while there is evidence of progress with respect to the adoption of special needs children, we found disabled children, particularly children with serious emotional and psychological problems, to be at high risk for adoption disruption. Again, although there are relatively few adoption disruptions, more attention must be given to this issue as disruptions do little more than decrease the chance of eventual adoption.

Adoption cases vulnerable to disruption need careful study in order to determine possible causes. Disrupted adoption is devastating. Imagine children being placed into foster care because their parent(s) don't want them, are unable to care for them, or abuse them and then being rejected by a prospective adoptive family. This amounts to being twice victimized and should be avoided at all costs.

Increasing placements with relatives may promote permanency. There are serious questions, however, about whether relative placements lead to adoption. Relatives may adopt, and more of them appear to be adopting. Adoption by relatives is another issue that needs further exploration. For example, when faced with a choice, when is it better to place a child with a relative as compared to an adoptive home? What criteria should be used to make such decisions?

We found evidence suggesting that subsidies may be an important incentive for encouraging adoptions. It does not necessarily follow, however, that more subsidies lead to more adoptions. This issue needs to be examined swiftly and carefully in other states because of the significant amount of dollars going into it. Policymakers and child welfare professionals would also be well advised to consider how subsidies could be made more effective, particularly with underrepresented populations being placed for adoption. It would also be fruitful to explore other kinds of incentives that may be helpful in this area. For example, what might be the impact of providing fiscal incentives to child welfare workers to get more children adopted? Would this reduce the number of children relegated to permanent foster care and being raised by the government? Some carefully developed and researched experiments in this area might prove useful in answering these questions.

Finally, policymakers, child welfare professionals, and child advocates in the states need to develop policies and procedures that will expedite adoptions without trampling on the rights of natural birth parents.

REFERENCES

Barth, R. P.; Berry, M.; Yoshikami; R., Goodfield; R. K., and Carson, M. L. (1988). Predicting adoption disruption. *Social Work,* 33, 227–33.

Child Welfare League of America (CWLA). (1997). See Petit and Curtis.

Courtney, M. (1993). Standardized outcome evaluation of child welfare services out-of-home care: Problems and possibilities. *Children and Youth Services Review,* 15, 349–69.

Finch, S. J.; Fanschel, D.; and Grundy, J. F. (1991). *Data collection in adoption and foster care.* Washington, DC: Child Welfare League of America.

Flango. (1990). Agency and private adoptions, by state. *Child Welfare, 49*(3), 263–75.

Hairston, C. F.; and Williams, V. G. (1989). Black adoptive parents: How they view agency adoption practices. *Social Casework, 70*(9), 534–38.

Hearing before the Subcommittee on Human Resources. (1991). *Testimony given by Marcia Robinson Lowry, Children's Rights Project of the ACLU Foundation* (Serial 102–5). Washington, DC: U.S. Government Printing Office.

Hewlett, S.A. and West, C. (1998). *The war against parents: What we can do for America's beleaguered moms and dads.* Boston: Houghton Mifflin.

Maluccio, A. N.; Fein, E.; and Davies, I. P. (1994). Family reunification: Research findings, issues, and directions. *Child Welfare, 73*(5), 489–504.

Maluccio, A. N.; Warsh, R.; and Pine, B. A. (1993). Rethinking family reunification after foster care. *Community Alternatives, 5*(2), 1–17.

McDonald, T. P.; Lieberman, A. A.; Partridge S.; and Hornby, H. (1991). Assessing the role of agency services in reducing adoption disruptions. *Children and Youth Services Review, 13*(5–6), 425–38.

Michigan adoption factbook. (1991). Lansing,: Michigan Federation of Private Child and Family Agencies.

Michigan House Bill No. 4427. (1993).

North American Council on Adoptable Children (NACA). (1991). *The Adoption Assistance and Child Welfare Act of 1980 (Public Law 96–272). The first ten years.* St. Paul, MN: Author.

Petit, M. R.; and Curtis, P. A. (1997). *Child abuse and neglect: A look at the states, 1997 CWLA state book.* Washington, DC: CWLA Press.

Rodriguez, P.; and Meyer, A. S. (1990). Minority adoptions and agency practices. *Social Work, 35*(6), 528–31.

Rosenthal, J.; Groze, V.; and Curiel, H. (1990). Race, social class and special needs adoption. *Social Work, 35*(6), 532–39.

Tatara, T. (1993). *Characteristics of children in substitute and adoptive care.* Washington, DC: American Public Welfare Association.

The White House Office of the Press Secretary (1997, November 4). *A proclamation.* [on-line]. Available: http://www.acf.dhhs.gov/news/adopt_wh.htm.

Wulczyn and Goerge. (1992). Foster care in New York and Illinois: The challenge of rapid change. *Social Service Review, 66*(2), 278–92.

CHAPTER 5

Child Welfare and Delinquency: Between Compassion and Control

Hardly a day goes by without a report in the media about crime, particularly violent crime. Although the rates of serious crime committed by adults have declined recently, this is not the case for juveniles. Juvenile homicides, for example, skyrocketed between 1988 and 1994 and are now the leading cause of death for African American males under the age of twenty four. Fortunately, and despite the predictions by some that these offenses would continue to increase, they began to decline in the mid 1990s (Snyder, 1997, November). Nonetheless, the violent juvenile crime rates are intolerably high and are a major concern on the part of the public and elected public officials.

The public is deeply concerned about juvenile crime with many people fearful of being the victim of violent acts by young people (Schwartz et al., 1992; Steinhart, 1988). Policymakers are trying to address these concerns in two ways. First, they are supporting harsher penalties for juveniles and policies designed to treat juvenile offenders as adults. Second, and, unfortunately to a much lesser degree, they are supporting efforts aimed at identifying some of the causes of violent juvenile crime.

The Clinton administration is also sensitive to this issue. For example, U.S. Attorney General Janet Reno has emphasized the need "to combat the nation's rising tide of violent youth crime, now emerging as a top domestic issue of the 90s, with a 'certainty-of-punishment' combined with an 'opportunity-for-rehabilitation' " (Howard, 1993, March/April, p. 1).

Previous research on the causes of juvenile crime has considered the relationship between child abuse and delinquency. The issue studied was whether being a victim of child abuse and/or neglect increases the chance of being arrested as a juvenile (Widom, 1989a, 1989b). While this is an important issue to address, the present study is more specifically concerned with whether placement in substitute care for reasons of abuse and neglect leads to serious juvenile crime. Fortunately, Michigan's CSMIS information system allowed us to look at this issue.

BACKGROUND

Much has been written, discussed, and assumed about the relationship between child abuse and neglect and delinquency. What research there is suggests that children who are mistreated are more likely to become delinquent than children who are not. However, the assumption by many that child maltreatment causes delinquency and that we can specifically identify and predict which abused children will commit delinquent acts, including acts of violence, has yet to be made. Those who might be interested in or surprised by our conclusion that the cause and effect relationship between child abuse and neglect and delinquency and our ability to predict which abused children will commit serious delinquent acts as a result of being mistreated should review the literature and draw their own conclusions.

Testimony before Congress on child welfare recognizes a link between youth crime and prior abuse and neglect (U.S. Government Printing Office, 1989; 1990; 1991; 1992, May). This testimony supports studies pointing out "clearly and convincingly that childhood victimization increases the likelihood of delinquency, adult criminality, and violent adult behavior" (U.S. Government Printing Office, 1992, May, p. 92). This interrelationship was also recognized by the U.S. Advisory Board on Child Abuse and Neglect (1993, April) when they acknowledged that "Failure to prevent child abuse and neglect is costing taxpayers billions of dollars each year in measures associated with remediating delinquent and criminal behavior, urban unrest, drug abuse, severe mental illness, and family dysfunction" (p. 2).

It has long been argued that the child welfare system may be a breeding ground for future delinquents. It has also been argued that the boundaries between the child welfare and juvenile justice systems are not as distinct as one might think (Lerman, 1980). It has been suggested that whether a child enters the child welfare system or the juvenile justice system is often a function of how the child's behavior is defined. For instance, it is a simple matter to "redefine delinquent-type behaviors as 'acting out' or as a symptom of an emotional disturbance [special needs]" (Lerman, 1980, p. 286).

Unfortunately, relatively little credible data exists to shed light on the movement of children between these systems and for understanding what predicts transitions between, or keeping children within, them. In general, the literature focuses on how children in the child welfare system (for abuse/neglect or delinquency reasons) exhibit similar and multiple problem behaviors. Widom (1992, October), however, has written about how exposure to abusive and neglectful living environments prior to out-of-home care may have some effect on later development.

Rutter, Quinton, and Hill (1990) argue that early childhood separation experiences and placements into substitute care are significant predictors of poor social functioning in adulthood. In a separate study, Widom (1991) examined the effects out-of-home placements had on abused and neglected children and noted that while abuse and neglect can lead to criminal behavior, out-of-home "placement alone [does] not appear to increase risk of criminal behavior" (p. 195).

Although one placement may not be detrimental to abused and neglected children, multiple placements are significantly associated with criminality (Widom, 1991).

The best available evidence to date suggests that some, but not all, abused and neglected children become involved in delinquency and adult criminal behavior (U.S. Government Printing Office, 1992; Widom 1989a; 1989b; 1991; 1992, October). In addition, it has been reported that "being abused or neglected as a child increases a person's risk for an arrest as a juvenile by 53 percent, as an adult by 38 percent and for violent crimes by 38 percent" (U.S. Government Printing Office, 1992, May, p. 96). These findings have also been confirmed by two later studies (Maxfield and Widom, 1996; Smith and Thornberry, 1995), showing that childhood victims of abuse or neglect are more likely to have a juvenile or adult arrest for any nontraffic offense (49 percent vs. 38 percent for control group for control group) and violent offense (18 percent vs. 14 percent).

STUDY OVERVIEW

This chapter describes a study that examined child welfare and delinquency career patterns for male children removed from their homes and placed into substitute care in Michigan's child welfare system. The study broadly defined the child welfare system to include abused/neglected male children and delinquents committed to the custody of the state. In particular, the study examined what differentiated male children who stayed in the child welfare system without becoming delinquent from those who turned delinquent.

We excluded females from this study because they represented a very small proportion of delinquent youth committed to state custody in Michigan. Although females were excluded from this analysis, we examined what little data we had on this population and we feel there are a number of issues that need careful and immediate attention. For example, the few female cases we looked at informally and were found to have experienced many more placements and much longer lengths of stay in the system as compared to the male cases. In addition, other data suggests that many young females are committed to the Michigan Family Independence Agency (FIA) as delinquents for relatively minor offenses. Again, this is particularly the case when compared to their male counterparts.

Our study of male children was designed with two phases. The first phase identified four distinct groups of children exhibiting various child welfare career patterns defined by their legal status. We defined children who were temporary or permanent state wards for reasons of abuse and/or neglect as "child welfare" (CW) cases. Children who were under state care and supervision for violation(s) of the delinquency codes were defined as "delinquent" (D) cases. Accordingly, the four groups were as follows: (1) children who started as child welfare cases and maintained a child welfare status during their system careers (CW); (2) children who started as child welfare cases and became delinquent (CW-D); (3) children who started as delinquents and maintained a delinquency status (D); and (4) children who started as delinquents and became child welfare cases (D-CW). The demographic characteristics of each group were examined along a number of dimensions including age, average lengths of stay in placements, legal status at first placement, number of placements, race, and type of placements.

The second phase of this study focused exclusively on delinquency careers (i.e., D and CW-D). In particular, we examined whether specific career patterns could be identified and which explanatory variables predicted those patterns. The main explanatory variables used in the study included the age at first placement, the number of previous placements, and race.

The study's two-phase structure allowed for a comprehensive examination of selected research questions and hypotheses. Specifically, the study explored three basic questions: (1) for children who did not experience a transition in legal status between child welfare and delinquency (CW and D), what variables predicted the probability of entering the system as a delinquent (D)? (2) or children who started with a child welfare legal status (CW and CW-D), what variables predicted the probability of shifting to a delinquent legal status (CW-D)? and (3) were there differences in the severity and types of offenses in each delinquency group (CW-D and D)?

With regard to the last question, there is a popular assumption that children in the child welfare system who "turn sour" (i.e., become delinquent) will exhibit more severe acting out behavior than children starting their careers as delinquents. The logic of this hypothesis lies in the possible effects of child maltreatment and multiple out-of-home placements on some children. These effects seem evident especially when children experience a series of relatively short-term placements which prohibit the development of social and emotional ties with significant others (adults as well as peers).

RESEARCH DESIGN

This study used a random sample of 20 percent of all male children entering the FIA child welfare system between October 10, 1980 and September 1, 1989 for abuse/neglect or delinquency.

Delinquent youth were referred and committed to FIA custody (the state youth corrections authority). Our data did not include juveniles placed under the custody of county probation departments and county-level correctional placements. However, state-level commitments to FIA are generally thought to be more serious and chronic offenders than are those typically kept and supervised at the county level.

This study examined each case according to the legal status at initial placement into substitute care and thereafter. Accordingly, each case was placed into one of the four groups previously defined (CW, CW-D, D, and D-CW). Because the D-CW group (those cases that shifted from a delinquent status to a child welfare status) was so small in number (about 0.2 percent of the total sample), we eliminated it from our analyses. The small proportion of D-CW children suggests that movement from a delinquency status to a nondelinquency child welfare status is a relatively rare event.

As noted previously, we designed this study with two phases. In the first phase (and after eliminating the D-CW group), we constructed and tracked three groups (CW, D, and CW-D), which allowed us to follow movements between FIA child welfare and delinquency placements. In the second phase, we examined the delinquent groups (D and CW-D) in detail. The study examined first-offense severity and its relationship to a child's previous FIA child welfare history. This design allowed us to detect identifiable career patterns. A career pattern might be a movement over time to more severe offenses, a movement to less severe offenses, or the tendency for different populations to develop unique patterns altogether. This study used two logistic regression models to explore the relationship between select explanatory and outcome variables. The outcome variables measured the probability of being in a certain group (D or CW-D) for different at-risk populations. For those children who did not make a legal status transition between the delinquency and child welfare systems (CW and D), the first model measured the probability of a child being in the D group. For those children who started as child welfare cases (CW and CW-D), the second model measured the probability of making a legal status transition (CW-D).

The explanatory variables used in this study included age, number of placements, and race. We selected these variables because they were identified as being relevant in the literature and because of their potential for being policy-relevant.

Race, as an explanatory variable, consisted of Caucasians, African Americans, and Others (Hispanics, Native Americans and those of other and unknown races and ethnicities). Age referred to a child's age at first placement into substitute care. Living arrangement at first placement included seven categories into which FIA initially placed children: (1) home-like arrangements (adoptive homes, independent living arrangements, a legal guardian's home, and parental home); (2) placement with relatives; (3) publicly-operated foster care; (4) privately-operated foster care; (5) short/long-term care institutions (group homes, public shelter home/facility, residential care center, private child caring institution, court treatment facility, and boarding schools); (6) correctional institutions (FIA camps, detention centers, jails, and training schools); and (7) other settings (AWOL, mental health facilities, and out-of-state placements).

Phase 1 Findings

The study's first phase revealed some interesting findings regarding the three groups (CW, CW-D, and D) under examination. The randomized sample's distribution closely resembled that of the child welfare population with respect to dependent variables, greatly increasing our confidence regarding the ability to generalize the findings. The distribution of the three groups (see table 5-1) was as follows: the D group constituted 31.6 percent of the total sample; the CW group constituted 66.2 percent; and the CW-D group constituted only 2.2 percent.

Table 5-1
Male Children by Race and Legal Status at First Placement

	Delinquency	Child Welfare	Child Welfare to Delinquency	Total
Race				
Caucasians	1,214	2,540	104	3,858
	[54.4%]	[54.3%]	[66.3%]	[54.6%]
	(31.5%)	(65.9%)	(2.7%)	(100%)
African American	961	1,950	44	2,955
	[43.1%]	[41.7%]	[28.0%]	[41.8%]
	(32.5%)	(66.0%)	(1.5%)	(100%)
Other	55	184	9	248
	[2.5%]	[3.9%]	[5.7%]	[3.5%]
	(22.2%)	(74.2%)	(3.6%)	(100%)
Total	2,230	4,674	157	7,061
	[100%]	[100%]	[100%]	[100%]
	(31.6%)	(66.2%)	(2.2%)	(100%)

Notes:
The chi-square statistic for Table 5-1 ($X^2 = 24.58$ with 4 degrees of freedom) is significant at the .001 level. All brackets contain column percentages. All parentheses contain row percentages. The Other category represents Hispanics/Latinos, Native Americans, and those of other and unknown races and ethnicities.

These results indicate that a very small percentage of children cross over from the child welfare system to the state-level delinquency system. It is important to remember that county-level delinquency adjudications and correctional placements are not included in this analysis. Nonetheless, it is encouraging that out-of-home, cross system shifts from child welfare to delinquency are relatively rare in Michigan.

Race

As seen in table 5-1, the proportions of African Americans, Caucasians, and Others in both the CW and D categories were consistent with their respective representations in the overall sample. Interestingly, issues of overrepresentation and underrepresentation became evident in the smaller CW-D category. Although Caucasians represented 54.6 percent of the total sample, they represented 66.3 percent of all children in the CW-D category. This indicated their overrepresentation in this career pattern. Conversely, African American were underrepresented in the CW-D category. While they represented 41.8 percent of the total sample, they represented 28.0 percent of the CW-D category. The association between race and career group was significant, which means the distribution of various racial groups was not random (X^2= 24.58 with 4 df; p <= .001).

These findings should be considered in light of the racial and ethnic composition of all children in Michigan. For example, African Americans represented about 17 percent and Caucasians represented approximately 79 percent of all children under eighteen years of age in Michigan in 1990 (Michigan League for Human Services, 1992). In short, this means that African Americans were substantially overrepresented in the total sample and in each career pattern category. In contrast, Caucasians were underrepresented in the total sample and each career category. The disparate treatment of children of color in both the child welfare and juvenile justice systems is a major concern nationally and is a serious issue in Michigan. It is one that warrants attention by policymakers and professionals in both systems.

Age

Michigan's juvenile court jurisdiction begins at age ten and ends at age seventeen. Accordingly, as expected, 98.3 percent (2,192/2,230) of D-group males experienced initial placements after age twelve. In the CW group, 79.5 percent (3,714 of 4,674) experienced initial placement before age twelve. After twelve years of age, only 20.5 percent (958 of 4,674) of the males were admitted as child welfare cases. In the CW-D group, 86 percent (135 of 157) changed status between ages nine and sixteen. For all males placed in delinquency groups (CW-D and D) after age twelve, 70 percent (2280 of 3238) were initially delinquency placements. These findings suggest that Michigan is willing to choose relatively compassionate (child welfare) options for children under age twelve while exercising control options (juvenile corrections) for male children age twelve and older.

Legal Status at First Placement

Table 5-2 examines the relationship between first placement living arrangements and legal status. Of all males initially placed at home, 59.1 percent were D-group members. The percentage of males initially living at home varied across the three groups with 27.4 percent of all D group males in this arrangement followed by the CW group (8.8 percent) and the CW-D group (6.4 percent). The fact that a larger proportion of D group children experienced home placements first is understandable because it was their behavior, not abuse or neglect at home, that had led them to state-level FIA involvement. As expected, a large percentage (55.7 percent) of D group males had initial placements in correctional settings. For CW males, public and private foster care placements were the categories with the largest proportion of placements collectively accounting for over 57 percent of all first placements. As table 5-2 indicates, the CW-D group possesses two large categories—public foster care and child caring institutions. Of these two categories, a larger proportion of CW-D children initially lived in public foster care (38.9 percent) as compared to child caring institutions (30.6 percent).

Table 5-2
First Placement Living Arrangements by Legal Status at First Placement

	Delinquency	Child Welfare	Child Welfare to Delinquency	Total
Living Arrangement				
Home-like Arrangements	610	412	10	1,032
	[27.4%] (59.1%)	[8.8%] (39.9%)	[6.4%] (1.0%)	[14.6%] (100%)
Relatives	48	770	14	832
	[2.2%] (5.8%)	[16.5%] (92.5%)	[8.9%] (1.7%)	[11.8%] (100%)
Foster Care (Public)	117	1,667	61	1,845
	[5.2%] (6.3%)	[35.7%] (90.4%)	38.9%] (3.3%)	[26.1%] (100%)
Foster Care (Private)	17	1,013	22	1,052
	[0.8%] (1.6%)	[21.7%] (96.3%)	[14.0%] (2.1%)	[14.9%] (100%)
Short/Long Term Care Institutions	193	763	48	1,004
	[8.7%] (19.2%)	[16.3%] (76.0%)	[30.6%] (4.8%)	[14.2%] (100%)
Correctional Facilities	1,220	6	1	1,227
	[54.7%] (99.4%)	[0.1%] (0.5%)	[0.6%] (0.1%)	[17.4%] (100%)
Other	25	43	1	49
	[1.1%] (36.2%)	[0.9%] (62.3%)	[0.6%] (1.5%)	[1.0%] (100%)
Total	**2,230**	**4,674**	**157**	**7,061**
	[100%] (31.6%)	[100%] (66.2%)	[100%] (2.2%)	[100%] (100%)

Notes:
Living arrangement at first placement included seven categories into which MDSS initially placed children (see first column and further description in the text). All brackets contain column percentages. All parentheses contain row percentages.

Average Length of Stay and Number of Placements

The three groups differed in number of placements and average lengths of stay (ALOS). The CW group had an average of 2.4 placements with an ALOS of 358 days. The D group had, on average, 4.1 placements with an ALOS of 198 days. The CW-D group had a relatively high average number of placements (7.3) with an ALOS of 245 days. In sum, children making a legal status transition from child welfare to delinquency stay in the system longer than do delinquents. They also experience more placements than the other groups studied.

PHASE 2 FINDINGS

The second phase of our study focused solely on the delinquent population. The study examined differences between the D group and the CW-D group. Over 27 percent (n=649) of males classified as delinquent did not have a recorded commitment offense (26.8 percent [n=597] in the D group and 33.1 percent [n=52] in the CW-D group). There are a number of possible explanations for delinquents entering the system without a recorded commitment offense. It is conceivable that their commitment offense was simply not recorded (missing data). Another possibility is that their charges may have been dropped.

Further analysis revealed that 43.6 percent (n=260) of D group males without a recorded commitment offense were placed at home. This finding suggests that these cases did not pose a serious threat to public safety. Another 21 percent (n=125) were in detention, and it remains unclear why they had no recorded commitment offense.

Contrary to our original hypothesis, there was no statistically significant difference (the z-test was not significant at the .05 level) between D group and CW-D group members regarding the frequency of different committing offenses. Furthermore, we found no statistically significant differences when we categorized commitment offenses according to misdemeanors, specific felony crimes (person and property), and status offenses (e.g., truancy and incorrigibility). Emerging patterns did suggest, however, that over 70 percent of commitment offenses in both groups were felony offenses. This was not particularly surprising given that we expected serious commitment offenses for state-level placements. Still, differences between groups did surface when offenses were examined more closely. While 40 percent of D group males had violent commitment offenses, only 24 percent of CW-D group males had such commitment offenses.

Another aspect of delinquent career patterns emerged when comparing groups according to first and subsequent offenses. The data indicated that a relatively small proportion (9.6 percent) of D group males had delinquent careers that escalated in offense severity. Sixty-four percent had nonescalating or deescalating careers; that is, they continued to commit additional crimes that tended to be as severe or less severe than the initial committing offense. In our analysis of delinquency career patterns for the this group, all 157 children in the this group who had their first offenses recorded did not have a subsequent offense entered into CSMIS.

Multivariate Analysis

This study used two logistic regression models to determine what predicted the likelihood of entering a delinquency group for various populations at risk (see table 5-3). The results for Model 1 (table 5-3) suggested that for those children who did not experience a transition in legal status (CW and D), age, number of placements, and race explained 25 percent of the variation in the outcome variable (whether a child was CW or D). As age and number of placements increased, so did the probability of becoming delinquent (see Model 1 in table 5-4). Being African American also increased a child's chance of being in the delinquent group (see Model 1 in table 5-4).

Table 5-3
Estimated Regression Coefficients for Logistic Regression Model

Dependent Variable Independent Variable	Model 1 Delinquency (N=3,734)	Model 2 Child Welfare to Delinquency (N=4,831)
Race		
Caucasian	0.3582 (2.5774)	-0.6381 (2.7449)
African American	0.5424 (5.7894)	-1.1619* (8.2222)
Age		
9-11	Not Applicable	2.1537* (54.998)
12-16	3.8689* (360.85)	2.3177*** (76.826)
17+	5.0564* (341.94)	-2.6476 (0.0743)
Number of Placements		
	0.2768* (200.95)	0.3706* (217.53)
	Pseudo R^2 #=0.25	Pseudo R^2 #=0.09

Notes:
1. The dependent variable (Y) was coded as follows: for Model 1, Y=1 if the child was in the D group, and Y=0 if he was in the CW group; for Model 2, Y=1 if the child was in the CW-D group, and Y=0 if he was in the CW group. Model 1 only examined children age 9 and older. Model 2 studied all children. The contrast group for both models included cases with a "child welfare" legal status throughout their careers in the system. Because Michigan's juvenile court jurisdiction begins at age 10, Model 1 examined children age 9 and older. 2. Reference groups: Race = other; Age = 9-11 for Model 1; and, Age = less than 9 for Model 2. 3. All parentheses contain Wald Chi-square statistics. * denotes significance at the .05 level for a two-tailed test. # Pseudo R^2 = c/(N + c), where c is the model chi-square and N is the total sample size.

Table 5-4
Predicted Probabilities for Delinquency Models

Dependent Variable– Delinquency Models Selected Groups	Model 1 Delinquency (N=3,734)	Model 2 Child Welfare to Delinquency (N=4,831)
All	0.5712	0.0096
Race		
Caucasian	0.5548	0.0116
African American	0.5997	0.0069
Other	0.4656	0.0216
Age		
Less than 9	N/A	0.0047
9–11	0.0459	0.0390
12–16	0.6973	0.0457
17+	0.8831	0.0003
Number of Placements		
1	0.3974	0.0054
2	0.4652	0.0079
3	0.5343	0.0113
5	0.6662	0.0235
10	0.8884	0.1331

Notes:
This study used the estimated regression coefficients for each model in table 5-3 to calculate the respective predicted probabilities in table 5-4. Predicted probabilities for each model with "all" explanatory variables controlled at their means.

As table 5-4 indicates, African Americans had a higher chance (about 60 percent) of being in the delinquent group as compared to Caucasians, who only had a 55.5 percent chance of being in this group, and Others, who had a 46.6 percent chance. The difference between the categories of Caucasians and Others was not statistically significant, but the difference between African Americans and Others was (see Model 1 for table 5-3).

The second logistic regression model examined legal status transitions for children who began their careers in the child welfare system (CW and CW-D). The findings (see Model 2 in table 5-3) suggested that the best single predictors of movement from child welfare to delinquency (CW-D) were age and number of placements.

Children in the nine to eleven and twelve to sixteen age groups were most at risk of making a legal status transition from child welfare to delinquency. The probabilities in Model 2 (table 5-4) indicate that both age groups would have about a 4 percent chance of making this shift (CW-D). The relationship between age and the probability of shifting between legal statuses was significant (p<.05). The low probabilities for children under age nine and over age sixteen is probably due to the fact that Michigan's age of juvenile court jurisdiction begins at age ten and ends at age seventeen.

We also found a positive linear relationship between the number of placements and the chances for movement into delinquency. As the number of placements increased, so did the probability of making the shift from child welfare to delinquency. Although race was a statistically significant predictor of this shift for African-American children as compared to Others (See Model 2 in table 5-3), the actual impact upon the chances of such shifts was negligible (see Model 2 in table 5-4).

DISCUSSION AND POLICY IMPLICATIONS

This chapter examined the career patterns of male children under the care and supervision of FIA. Specifically, it focused on the legal status of placements, the demography of children in different system career patterns, and the factors that differentiated male children placed with a legal status of abuse and neglect from children placed with a delinquent legal status. The main findings were as follows:

- The majority of male children in state-level substitute care were placed with an abuse/neglect legal status;

- As a child's age increased, his chances of experiencing a delinquency status placement increased (CW-D or D);

- Only 2.2 percent of male children in the sample began in state-level placements with an abuse/neglect legal status and shifted into state-level placements with a delinquent legal status (CW-D);

- The number of children who initially began with a delinquent status and shifted into a child welfare (nondelinquent) status at the state level was negligible (0.2 percent).

The data from Model 1 indicated that the best single predictors of delinquency placements (D) among males were: (1) being African American; (2) being older; and (3) having had a higher number of placements when compared to males who remained in the child welfare system. For Model 2, children who crossed over from a child welfare to a delinquency status (CW-D) clearly had more placements than children in other groups. This finding is consistent with previous research that shows that a history of multiple/serial placements was associated with delinquent and criminal behavior (Widom, 1991). Clearly, efforts should be made to prevent children from experiencing multiple placements. Unlike previous research (Widom, 1991), this study moved beyond arrests as an outcome measure and used actual state-level placements or commitments as an outcome measure. In general, children who crossed over (CW-D) resembled delinquents more than nondelinquents in terms of age at first placement and average length of stay. In addition, the average length of stay in a particular placement was roughly half as long for delinquents (198 days) as compared to nondelinquents (358 days).

For children with an initial child-welfare status (CW and CW-D), those between age nine and age sixteen were most at risk of experiencing later shifts to a delinquency status (CW-D). For example, the chances of children between age nine and age eleven to make a legal status transition (CW-D) were seven times higher than the chances for children under age nine.

When offense severity was compared for the two delinquent groups (CW-D and D), there were no significant differences found in first commitment offense. In general, over 70 percent of delinquents studied entered the system with an associated felony offense. Children who crossed over from child welfare to delinquency (CW-D) tended to commit fewer crimes against persons.

This finding did, in part, contradict propositions put forward by Widom (1992) regarding the cycle of violence. First, our findings did not corroborate the idea that children with an abuse/neglect status are significantly more likely to be serious violent offenders as evidenced by state-level commitments for such acts. However, difficulty in interpreting the discrepant results may be due (at least in part) to the lack of CSMIS data about prior history for those who entered as delinquents. As stated earlier, commitment to FIA tends to occur when a youth has committed a serious violent crime (aggravated assault, armed robbery, murder, or rape) or is a chronic repeater. Many of the males tracked in this study may have begun their delinquency careers at the county level before state-level intervention commenced, but this delinquency activity would not show up in our data. Therefore, the severity and chronicity of a child's offense history did not necessarily start with the commitment data to which we had access.

Why are older children more likely to enter the system as delinquents? There are a number of considerations that need to be taken into account to understand this question. On the surface, it appeared that children under age twelve were managed with "kid gloves." That is, it appeared as though younger children received state-level intervention for abuse/neglect protection. On the other hand, the age of criminal responsibility (which begins at age ten in Michigan) dictated that younger children were unlikely to enter the state care system with a delinquency status because they simply did not qualify legally. Additionally, Michigan's children must be at least age twelve to be placed into training schools and youth rehabilitation camps.

Nonetheless, there is a larger issue to consider here. Results indicated that a large proportion of children who entered the child welfare system after age twelve were labeled delinquent. It appeared as though compassion for children ended at the age of "delinquent responsibility." After that, compassion tended to convert into social control. This finding was even more pronounced given that there are no age limitations for child welfare placements as there are for delinquency placements.

What was it about this particular age that separated children protected by the state from those punished by the state? On the surface, the answer may require us to reexamine the meaning attached to behavior. The following questions arise from this study: Is there something older children do that makes them substantially different from their younger counterparts? Do older children exhibit similar behaviors that become classified as delinquent? Or, perhaps, is it possible that older children are unlikely (less likely) to be abused and neglected? An examination of these questions calls for research that is beyond the scope of this chapter. However, these are critical questions and should receive priority attention from academics, child advocates, lawyers, policymakers, politicians, and practitioners in both the child welfare and juvenile justice systems.

The overrepresentation of children of color in both the child welfare and juvenile justice systems is well documented (Mech, 1983; Krisberg, Schwartz, and Fishman, 1987). Nevertheless, severe limitations with this data make it difficult to know why this overrepresentation occurs. For example, this study explored the experience of children in the "Other" race category, a category that includes children from a wide variety of racial and ethnic backgrounds who may have very different experiences in these systems. For instance, Native American and Hispanic children may not have similar child welfare experiences, but our data would not reflect these differences. Our study was able to identify clear distinctions between the representation of African American and Caucasian children in both child welfare and juvenile justice systems as compared to their representations in the general population. Clearly, policymakers and practitioners seeking to reduce the child welfare and delinquency populations in Michigan need to carefully examine and better understand why there is such high overrepresentation of African-American children.

Still other concerns remain unaddressed. There is a growing national problem characterized by the oversimplification of debates regarding foster care's potentially harmful consequences. An article in the *Detroit Free Press* (Kresnak, 1993, May 28), which discussed FIA's concerns about the risks of placing children in foster care, noted that "studies have shown that children in foster care are more likely to commit crimes and land in juvenile training schools or, as adults, in prison" (p.11A).

While this may be true, it oversimplifies the issues and misleads the public. The quote implies that foster care is a breeding ground for serious juvenile crime and increases a child's chances of entering training schools and adult prisons. As noted in the previous literature review, it is not necessarily foster care that leads to juvenile crime and incarceration. However, unstable living arrangements characterized by multiple placements may be the real or major culprit here. In other words, the child welfare system is not necessarily a breeding ground for delinquency in the same way as many may think. The implications are clear: policymakers and child welfare professionals should begin to develop effective protocols and procedures to prevent placements in potentially unstable environments. Moreover, they should do everything possible to prevent placements initially thought to be stable from unraveling and destabilizing.

REFERENCES

Howard, B. (1993, March/April). Reno targets violent youth crime. *Youth Today: The Newspaper on Youth Work,* pp. 1, 4–5.

Kresnak, J. (1993, May 28). Must kids pay to save the family? Prosecutors fear DSS policy poses threat to children. *Detroit Free Press,* p. 11A.

Krisberg, B.; Schwartz, I. M.; and Fishman, G. (1987). The incarceration of minority youth. *Crime & Delinquency,* 33, 173–205.

Lerman, P. (1980). Trends and issues in the deinstitutionalization of youths in trouble. *Crime & Delinquency, 26*(3), 281–98.

Maxfield, G. M., and Widom, C. S. (1996). The cycle of violence: Revisited 6 years later. *Archives of Pediatric Adolescent Medicine* 150, 390–95.

Mech, E. V. (1983). Out-of-home placement rates. *Social Service Review, 57*(4), 659–67.

Michigan League for Human Services. (1992). *Michigan kids count 1992 data book: County profiles of child and family well-being.* Lansing: Michigan League for Human Services.

Rutter, M.; Quinton, D.; and Hill, J. (1990). Adult outcome of institution-reared children: Males and females compared. In L. Robins & M. Rutter (Eds.), *Straight and devious pathways from childhood to adulthood* (pp. 135–57). Cambridge, MA: Cambridge University Press.

Schwartz, I. M. (1989). *(In)justice for juveniles: Rethinking the best interests of the child.* Lexington, MA: Lexington Books.

Schwartz, I. M.; Kerbs, J. J.; Hogston, D. M.; and Guillean, C. L. (1992). *Combating juvenile crime: What the public really wants.* Ann Arbor: Center for the Study of Youth Policy, University of Michigan School of Social Work.

Smith, C. and Thornberry, T.P. (1995) The relationship between childhood maltreatment and adolescent involvement in delinquency. *Criminology, 33*(4), 451–81.

Snyder, H. (1997, November). Juvenile arrests 1996. *Juvenile Justice Bulletin.* Washington, DC: U.S. Department of Justice, Office of Justice Programs, Office of Juvenile Justice and Delinquency Prevention.

Steinhart, D. (1988). *N.C.C.D. FOCUS California opinion poll: Public attitudes on youth crime.* San Francisco: National Council on Crime and Delinquency.

U.S. Advisory Board on Child Abuse and Neglect. (1993, April). *The continuing child protection emergency: A challenge to the nation.* Washington, DC: U.S. Government Printing Office.

U.S. Government Printing Office. (1989). Programs and services designed to prevent unnecessary foster care placement. Hearings before the Subcommittee on Human Resources of the Committee on Ways and Means, House of Representatives (Serial 101–13). Washington, DC: Author.

U.S. Government Printing Office. (1990). Federally funded child welfare, foster care, and adoption assistance programs. Hearing before the Subcommittee on Human Resources of the Committee on Ways and Means, House of Representatives (Serial 101–90). Washington, DC: Author.

U.S. Government Printing Office. (1991). Child Abuse, Domestic Violence, Adoption and Family Services Act of 1991 (Senate Report 102–64). Washington, DC: Author.

U.S. Government Printing Office. (1992, May). Urban America's need for social services to strengthen families. Hearing before the Subcommittee on Human Resources of the Committee on Ways and Means, House of Representatives (Serial 102–110). Washington, DC: Author.

Widom, C. S. (1989a). Child abuse, neglect, and adult behavior: Research design and findings on criminality, violence and child abuse. *American Journal of*

Widom, C. S. (1989b). The cycle of violence. *Science*, 244, 160–66.
Widom, C. S. (1991). The role of placement experiences in mediating the criminal consequences of early childhood victimization. *American Journal of Orthopsychiatry*, *61*(2), 195–209.
Widom, C. S. (1992, October). The cycle of violence. *National Institute of Justice: Research in Brief.* Washington, DC: U.S. Department of Justice.

CHAPTER 6

The Role of Residential Care

Policymakers are concerned about the growing number of children in out-of-home placements. Rarely, however, are out-of-home placements carefully defined and differentiated. For example, references to the child welfare system and to foster care often fail to identify and discuss the different types of substitute care and their impact on children's lives. This is an important issue because not all out-of-home placements are the same. Different types of placement options are expected to perform different functions. For example, shelter care is supposed to be a relatively short-term placement option that can be provided in a family home or a small residential facility. Children are usually placed into shelter care for a very short time until more permanent plans can be made for them.

Placement types also differ significantly with respect to cost, level of restrictions, and types of cases they may serve. Some of the most costly and restrictive types of placements are in child caring institutions (e.g., group homes and residential treatment facilities). Although only about 17 percent of the children living in substitute care nationally in 1989 were living in group homes, emergency shelter facilities, or other types of child caring facilities such as residential treatment centers (Tatara, 1993), these institutions play an important role in state and local child welfare service delivery systems.

Despite the important role these institutions play, no one knows precisely how many children there are in these facilities, how many children are placed into them annually, and how long they stay in them. Equally important, no one knows how effective these facilities are or what happens to the children who were placed in them once they leave or are discharged. Although it is difficult to imagine, there are no accurate and reliable statistics regarding the total number of children in residential care nationally. Also, relatively little is known about these facilities and what actually happens to the children who are placed in them. A study by Edwards (1994) highlights what little is known about these programs. As this study notes, most of the data on children in residential care refers to treatment facilities for emotionally disturbed youth. Even this data is often incomplete and confusing. The findings generally refer to mental health facilities and usually do not include many of the small and large institutions that house dependent, abused, and neglected children. Moreover, juvenile delinquents housed in residential programs are rarely included.

The inconsistencies in the published figures are quite dramatic. For example, Durkin and Durkin (1975) reported that there were about 150,000 children and adolescents in 200 childcare institutions. In 1983, a national study found that there were 368 residential treatment facilities (RTF) for children and adolescents in the United States with a one-day count of 18,276 residents (Papenfort, Young, and Dore, 1988). This number is roughly consistent with Wells (1991), who reported that there were 19,215 children in residential facilities at the end of 1983. A 1990 study by the U.S. House Select Committee on Children, Youth, and Families reported that there were 25,334 children in residential facilities. The only conclusion one can draw from this data is that "exact numbers are difficult to assess, however the number of children and adolescents in residential treatment is substantial" (Edwards, 1994, p. 88).

There are many reasons for the discrepancies in the numbers. The most obvious is a result of different studies looking at different types of facilities. Child caring facilities and the types of children they may serve do not always fit into clearly defined categories. For example, residential facilities are often categorized by the most common diagnosis or problems of the children they serve (e.g., emotionally disturbed, substance abuse, and delinquent). Many child caring facilities serve dependent and neglected, physically and sexually abused, and delinquent youth at the same time. Also, many of the children housed in residential care exhibit multiple problems. Another important reason for the discrepancies is that collecting data on institutionalized children has never been a priority. Until it is, we will probably never know how many children are housed in these facilities and what happens to them when they are there and after they leave. Also, the fact that children are housed in public, not-for-profit, and for-profit facilities further complicates the situation. The for-profit sector, particularly in-patient psychiatric and substance abuse treatment facilities, has been very reluctant to publish and share its data on child and adolescent admissions.

We attempted to estimate the number of juveniles in child caring institutions by analyzing data furnished by the Children' Defense Fund. The data consists of unpublished statistics collected by the U.S. Bureau of Census for the year 1990. Their figures indicate that there were 265,191 children under the age of eighteen in residential care on the day the census was taken. Of these, 27 percent (n=72,761) were children in residential facilities for delinquents, (e.g., public and private training schools, detention centers, jails, police lockups, halfway houses, and other similar types of juvenile institutions). There were 25,840 children (9.7 percent) in psychiatric hospitals or residential treatment centers for emotionally disturbed children, and 20,854 (7.9 percent) children in homes for the abused dependent and neglected. While the 265,191 figure may be the best available, research completed by the Center for the Study of Youth Policy at the University of Pennsylvania suggests it is probably conservative. The center has been carefully and systematically studying the numbers of juveniles in facilities for delinquents for more than a decade. It's findings, utilizing the U.S. Census Bureau's Biennial Survey of Children in Public and Private Youth Detention and Correction Facilities, indicate that the number of children reported to be in delinquency facilities is conservative and may underestimate the actual number by as much as 25 percent.

RESIDENTIAL CARE IN MICHIGAN: A CASE EXAMPLE

The research we conducted in Michigan is helpful in terms of understanding the dynamics of residential care. Of the 15,240 children in Michigan's out-of-home care in the first quarter of 1993, 2,796 (18 percent) were in private child care institutions, FIA training schools, FIA camps, mental health facilities, or court treatment facilities (Caldwell, 1993, May). Although far fewer children are in institutions than in foster homes, institutional costs accounted for slightly more than half of FIA's $183,073,888 out-of-home placement budget in fiscal year 1990 (Michigan Department of Social Services, 1992, February 25). Because FIA relies heavily on contracting with the private not-for-profit sector, most of the children who are institutionalized are housed in private group homes, residential treatment facilities, and youth correction institutions.

FIA has been, and continues to be, concerned about the high costs and questionable benefits of institutional care for children and youth. FIA staff have completed internal studies of recidivism and/or recycling in private child care institutions and looked for ways to reduce the number of children placed in this expensive care (Schwartz, 1994). This chapter focuses on which children (e.g., delinquent, emotionally disturbed, and abused and neglected) are likely to be placed in an institution and their chance of moving to a permanent home. More specifically, we look closely at temporary and permanent wards of the state who are placed into public and private institutions in Michigan. Given the risks of institutional placements, we wanted to know which children are placed in institutional care and how these placements affect their chance of moving to a permanent home. We addressed the following questions:

1.   Who are the children who begin their child welfare careers in institutions?

2.   What factors predict the chance of children moving into institutional care when they do not start out in institutional placements?

3.   What is the chance of a child placed in institutional care to be subsequently placed in a permanent home?

After discovering the significance of initially being placed in an institutional setting and the fact that children from Wayne County (which includes the city of Detroit) had a very high chance of beginning their child welfare careers in an institution, we also asked (4) What are the chances of achieving permanency for children whose first placement is an institution and how does the probability vary between Wayne and other counties?

Methodology

To answer the first question we used a multinomial logic regression model with first living arrangement as the dependent variable. The model measures the predicted probabilities of beginning in shelter care, institutional care or all other forms of care. Our definition of institution includes private child care institutions for delinquents and nondelinquents, mental health facilities, FIA group homes, FIA residential care centers, public training schools, FIA camps, court treatment facilities, and boarding schools. Although all of these facilities are included in our definition, the overwhelming majority of the children in this category are housed in private child care institutions that are privately operated, licensed residential treatment facilities. For independent variables, we considered how age at first placement, race, gender, county residence, and handicap status affected the chance of being placed in shelter care, institutional care, or some other living arrangement.

For the second and third question we used two statistical models of event history analysis. The results presented in this chapter come from a proportional hazards model (Cox model), which carefully captures the relationship between the immediate prior placement and the chances of moving into another type of placement from a dynamic perspective. In the Cox model, the probability of moving into an institution or permanent placement is shown by the hazard rate. The type of placement prior to a change is treated as a time-varying covariant (independent variable) in a continuous-time model.

The hazard rate, or hazard function, may be interpreted as the instantaneous probability that episodes in an interval of time (t, t+dt) are terminating, provided the event has not occurred before the beginning of this interval. To make the results easier to understand, we will refer to hazard or hazard rate as the transition rate, which shows the changing rate of transitions between different types of living arrangements, such as the transition from a noninstitutional to an institutional placement (question 2), or from a non-permanent to a permanent placement (question 3).

In studying questions 2 and 3, a discrete-time model was used; this allowed us to follow the children's movement on a quarterly basis. In other words, one can identify the types of placements that are more likely to lead to an institutional placement (question 2) or a permanent placement (question 3) within a three-month period. The results of these models closely match the results of the Cox model. As the discrete-time model findings are similar we only refer to them briefly in this chapter.

For the final question, we used a logistical regression model, employing "moving to a permanent living arrangement" as the dependent variable. The independent variables used here were the same as those used to answer question 1. We also used this model to look at the joint effect of first living arrangement and county on moving to permanency.

Although questions 3 and 4 both measure the chance of moving to permanency, we used different models and treated living arrangement variables differently in both instances. The Cox model in question 3 shows the transition rate for moving immediately into a permanent setting for each living arrangement.

The regression model for question 4 shows the chance of moving to a permanent setting within a period of four years depending on where a child started in the system.

For the models used to measure moving to a permanent setting (questions 3 and 4), the probability of moving from a temporary placement (i.e., foster care or an institution) to a permanent setting within a four-year period was calculated. A permanent setting was defined as own home, relative's home, legal guardian, adoptive home, or independent living.

The Study Samples

In addressing the research questions a 5 percent random sample of 37,049 children who entered Michigan's child welfare system between 1981 and 1987 was selected. The sample consisted of 1,794 cases of which 165 were first placed in shelter care, 205 started out in an institution and 1,424 started out in foster care, homes of relatives, adoptive homes, and, in a few instances, their own homes. The first placement distribution of the random sample closely resembles the distribution of first placements of the entire population; therefore, one can be reasonably confident about the generalizability of the sample study results to the entire population.

For the second question, who moves into institutional care, we followed the placement histories of children in the sample over a period of four years. As the focus here is on the movement of children from noninstitutional to institutional placements, those cases that started in institutional care were excluded from the analysis. As a result, the sample size that was relevant for this second question shrank to 1,589 children. Of these children, 151 (9.5 percent) had at least one previous placement in an institution.

For the population used to answer the third and fourth questions, who moves to a permanent placement, those children who started in a permanent placement were removed from our 5 percent sample. To simplify the study, we focused on the probability of moving to a permanent placement the first time within a four-year period. After removing the children who started in a permanent setting, the final sample for this analysis consisted of 1,386 children. Among these children, 55.7 percent (772) moved to a first permanent placement within the four-year window.

Who Are the Children Who Begin Their Child Welfare Careers in Institutions?

Children generally did not start their child welfare careers in institutions. In fact, children entering the child welfare system had only about a 7 percent chance of starting out in an institution. They were far more likely (p=.84) to start out in some kind of noninstitutional setting such as foster care, the home of relatives, an adoptive home or the home of legal guardians. They had a 9 percent chance of starting in shelter care (see table 6-1).

Although children were unlikely to start out in institutions, the predicted probabilities differed depending upon age at entry into the system, race, gender, county of residence, and handicap status (table 6-1). For example, older children had a much greater chance of starting out in an institution than did younger children. Males were more likely to be placed in institutions than were females; females were more likely to be placed in a shelter. Children with handicaps were slightly more likely to begin their careers in such facilities. African-American children were more likely to be placed in shelters than in institutional care as compared to Caucasian children.

Table 6-1
Predicted Probability of Being Initially Placed in Institutional Care
(Based on a Multinomial Logit Model)

	Shelter	Public/Private Institutions	Other Care
All	0.0864	0.0699	0.8438
Age			
0	0.0431***	0.0262***	0.9306
2	0.0613***	0.0291***	0.9096
5	0.0906***	0.0378***	0.8717
7	0.1075***	0.0484***	0.8441
10	0.1217***	0.0782***	0.8001
11	0.1221***	0.0944***	0.7835
12	0.1201***	0.1152***	0.7646
15	0.0988***	0.2204***	0.6807
17	0.0740***	0.3407***	0.5853
Race			
Caucasian	0.0673***	0.0803	0.8524
African American	0.1254***	0.0612	0.8134
Other	0.0943	0.0286	0.8770
Gender			
Female	0.0993*	0.0573**	0.8434
Male	0.0741*	0.0858**	0.8401
County			
Non-Wayne	0.1134***	0.0216***	0.8651
Wayne	0.0378***	0.3912***	0.5709
Handicap Status			
No	0.0850	0.0690***	0.8460
Yes	0.1016	0.0793***	0.8191

Notes:
* Significant at 0.1 level, two-tailed test; ** Significant at 0.05 level, two-tailed test; *** Significant at 0.01 level, two-tailed test.
"Other Care" is the reference group and its significance level cannot be shown. This category is mostly made up of family foster care placements but also includes placement at home, with relatives, with a legal guardian, or in an adoptive home.

Children entering the child welfare system in Wayne County had a particularly high risk of starting out in an institution. In fact, children from Wayne County had almost a seventeen times greater chance of starting out in an institution than did children from other counties in the state.

What Factors Predict the Probability for Children Who Do Not Start Out in Institutional Care of Moving into Such Placements?

According to the discrete-time model, in general, a child had only a .2 percent chance of moving into an institution each quarter year of the four-year period if he or she did not start with placement in institutional care. Table 6-2 presents estimated effects of explanatory variables on the transitional rate from the Cox model results. The relationship between age at first placement and the odds of being placed into institutional care was almost linear. A one-year increase in age at first placement increased the transition rate of moving into an institution by 28 percent.

Table 6-2
Estimated Effect of Explanatory Variables on the Transition Rate for Moving into Institutional Care
(Based on a Cox Model)

Covariates	Regression Coefficient B	Relative Risk exp(B)
Age	0.2489^{***}	0.0699
Race (Other is Reference)		
Caucasian	0.1598	1.1733
African American	-0.1203	0.8867
Gender (Female is Reference)		
Male	0.1885	1.2075
County (Non-Wayne is Reference)		
Wayne	1.5397^{***}	4.6631
Handicap (None is Reference)		
Handicap	0.2972	1.3460
Living Arrangements Prior to Change (Foster Care is Reference)		
Shelter	-0.0877	0.9161
Permanency	-2.5266^{***}	0.0799
Other (AWOL and out-of-state)	-0.9487	0.3872

Notes:
*** Significant at 0.01 level, two-tailed test. All Living Arrangement variables are time-varying.

The transition rate for moving into institutional care also differed by race and ethnicity. Caucasians had the greatest transition rate for moving into institutional care, followed by the ethnic category Other (Hispanics, Native Americans and those of other and unknown races or ethnicities) and then African Americans. The transition rate for Caucasians was 17 percent larger than that for the Other group. The transition rate for African Americans was 11.4 percent less than for the Other group.

Males were also more likely than females to move into institutional care; their transition rate was about 21 percent greater. There was also a substantial difference in the transition rate between children from Wayne and other counties. The transition rate for those living in Wayne County was 3.7 times larger than the rate for those living in other counties (p<.01). Furthermore, children with handicaps had a 35 percent larger transition rate than those without.

As far as living arrangement (i.e., type of placement prior to moving into residential care) is concerned, we found foster care more likely to lead to a subsequent placement in an institution. A permanent placement was the least likely to lead to an institutional care placement. The rank of placements according to their chances of leading to a subsequent move into institutional care (from most to least likely) was as follows: (1) foster care, (2) shelter care, (3) other living arrangement (out-of-state and AWOL—children who run away from a placement), and (4) a permanent placement. The transition rate for moving into an institution from a previous placement in shelter care was 8 percent less than the rate for a previous placement in foster care. The rate for other living arrangements was 61 percent less than that for foster care. And the rate for a permanent placement was 92 percent less than that for foster care. However, only the permanency variable was statistically significant (p <.01).

What Is the Chance for a Child Placed into an Institution to Be Subsequently Placed in a Permanent Environment? Does the Chance of Achieving Permanency Differ with Respect to Various Types of Placement Options?

Trends and patterns for achieving permanency have been discussed in other chapters and will not be repeated here. Instead, we will discuss the impact of institutions on the odds of achieving permanency. According to the discrete-time model (using three-month intervals), in general, a child had an 8.8 percent chance of moving into a permanent living arrangement within each quarter of the four-year period if she or he did not start out in such a placement.

It appears that shelter care placements were more likely to lead to permanency than institutional placements (see table 6-3). In fact, the transition rate for achieving permanency for shelter care was more than 150 percent larger than the rate for institutions (24.6 percent vs. 9.7 percent, respectively). However, both shelter care and institutions were less likely than foster care to achieve permanency. In addition, we found that even the children in the miscellaneous category (out-of-state and AWOL status) were more likely to have a subsequent permanent placement than were children placed in child caring institutions. The chances for out-of-state placements and children with an AWOL status to achieve a permanent placement was 135 percent larger than the rate for children placed in institutions. This suggests that children who run away and children from other states may be achieving permanency more often than children from Michigan who obediently stay in institutions.

In sum, the rank order of various living arrangements with respect to their chances of leading to a permanent placement was as follows: (1) foster care, (2) shelter care, (3) other, and (4) institutions.

Table 6-3
Estimated Effect of Living Arrangement on the Transition Rate
for Moving into Permanency (Based on a Cox Model)

Living Arrangements Prior to Change	Regression Coefficients B	Relative Risk exp (B)
(Foster Care is Reference)		
Shelter	-1.4008[***]	0.2464
Public/Private Institutions	-2.3325[***]	0.0971
Other (AWOL and out-of-state)	-1.4605[***]	0.2321

Notes:
[***] Significant at 0.01 level, two-tailed test. All Living Arrangement variables are time-varying. Other variables included in the model but not shown here are: age at first placement, race, gender, Wayne County or not, and handicap status.

What Are the Chances for a Child Who Starts Out in an Institution to Achieve Permanency?

In order to evaluate the impact of institutional care on Michigan's children, we looked at whether an initial residential placement would hurt a child's chances of moving to a permanent home. Some of the other factors that affect permanency were discussed in chapter 3.

It was pointed out in chapter 3 that a child's first living arrangement is an important predictor of future movement through the child welfare system. Because children in Wayne County had twenty times the chance of being placed initially into an institution, as compared to children in the rest of the state, we decided to explore how first placement and county of residence affect future movement. We were particularly interested in seeing whether and how Wayne County's extensive use of institutional care and permanency rate might be related.

A binary logistic regression model that treats the probability of moving to a permanent living arrangement as a dependent variable was used. This model allowed us to see how county and first living arrangement might jointly effect this probability.

In general, children who started in a nonpermanent living arrangement had about a fifty-fifty chance of moving to a permanent living arrangement within four years (see table 6-4). Those children initially placed in a temporary shelter had a better chance for this, while children placed initially into an institution had a much lower chance. This finding is consistent with the intended purposes of shelter and institutional care as a shelter is meant to be used only temporarily until a more stable environment is found and institutions are used for children who cannot be placed immediately in a permanent home.

Children in Wayne County, however, had a very different pattern. Wayne County children in shelter had the worst chance of moving to a permanent home. This finding raises serious questions about the use of shelters in Wayne County. In chapter 3 we reported that children in Wayne County had a low chance of achieving permanency. This may be due to the inappropriate use of shelter care and the overuse of institutional care in that county. When comparing children initially placed in institutions in Wayne County with those in the rest of the state, we see that children in Wayne County had a somewhat better chance of achieving permanency. However, starting in institutional settings diminished the chances for children achieving permanency irrespective of county of residence.

Table 6-4
Predicted Probability of Moving to Permanency
Controlling for County and First Living Arrangement
(Based on a Logistical Regression Model)

Variables	Probability	Percent Deviation
All	.5161	
Shelter	.6505	+26 percent
Other Substitute Care	.5206	+01 percent
Institutional Care	.3851	-25 percent
Wayne		
Shelter	.3806	-26 percent
Other Substitute Care	.5758	+11 percent
Institutional Care	.4289	-17 percent
Non-Wayne		
Shelter	.6380	+24 percent
Other Substitute Care	.5070	-02 percent
Institutional Care	.3722	-28 percent

Notes:
* All is the probability of moving into permanency holding all the independent variables at the mean. The Percent Deviation column shows the percentage difference of each probability from this mean.

DISCUSSION AND IMPLICATIONS

Institutions, particularly privately operated group homes and residential treatment centers, present a number of special challenges to child welfare administrators, elected public officials, and child advocates. There is clearly a need to figure out how to free up the bulk of the resources tied up these institutions so they can be used for less costly services. Although child caring institutions serve less than 20 percent of the children in out-of-home placements, they account for a disproportionate (40 percent to 50 percent) amount of all public child welfare out-of-home expenditures. This might not be so bad except for the fact that there is so little credible scientific evidence that such facilities are effective in treating and rehabilitating children. Moreover, as the data from Michigan suggests, the rates of recidivism in these institutions is extremely high (Schwartz, 1994). Our research also suggests that placement in these facilities decreases the chances for children to be placed subsequently in a permanent placement in comparison to other types of options.

Another challenge is to figure out which children really need to be housed or confined in residential centers. There are some young people who cannot be managed in less structured settings and must be housed in controlled environments. However, even in these instances, there is a need to determine what kinds of residential experiences are likely to be effective.

One question that must be asked is, Why has the residential care industry flourished, particularly in light of the absence of compelling data that such services are effective and lead to permanency? There are many possible explanations. For example, the criteria for referring children and youth to residential treatment are vague (e.g., "emotionally disturbed" or oppositional). This lack of precision, vagueness, and subjectivity make it possible to place almost any troubled child into a facility, including children who may have serious and chronic problems (delinquent and nondelinquent) as well as children who may not . This includes children who might benefit from a highly structured and self-contained program as well as those who might not. Children may also be placed into residential facilities because they are disobedient and social workers may not have the time and resources to work with them in the community. They may be placed because they cannot be controlled in a foster home. In some cases, they may be placed because a residential facility may have a "bed" available and it may be more convenient simply to send them away to an institution. There may also be pressures to remove troublesome youth from the community as is often the case with delinquents.

Administrators of residential treatment centers generally do a good job of marketing their services to juvenile and family court judges and to child welfare officials. They are usually members of state child care or residential treatment center associations that lobby and advocate on behalf of their constituents. These associations are primarily concerned with making sure their member organizations are paid enough for the services they provide to cover their expenses and that there are no significant interruptions to the flow of children into facilities. These associations tend to support less intrusive and less costly programs for children, but not if such programs or strategies are designed to reduce substantially the size of the residential care industry and hurt their constituents or members.

The proponents of residential care argue that their services are necessary and effective. They may even cite studies or produce what might appear to be impressive outcome or follow-up data on the children they served. Unfortunately, the studies they use to justify their programs tend to be seriously flawed and not very credible.

Our research clearly shows the odds for being placed into an institution are significantly greater for children in Wayne County than is the case for children in other jurisdictions in Michigan. In light of this, FIA officials would be well advised to develop a strategy specifically targeted towards Wayne County children.

The relationship between FIA and the private child welfare community is not the best. While they give the appearance of cooperating in public, there is a deep lack of trust between the two parties. Some FIA officials believe the private agencies, particularly those providing residential treatment services, are motivated, in large part, by receiving lucrative contracts. Some private agency staff think the state is mainly interested in bidding out all services and trying to provide the cheapest, and not necessarily the best, services possible. To make matters worse, FIA thinks it has the expertise to build an effective child welfare system, while many in the private sector see FIA in an entirely different light. In reality, FIA and the private not-for-profit sector need each other. It is hard to imagine having an enlightened twenty-first century child welfare system without an effective public-private partnership.

There are some important ways that the public and private sectors can cooperate. There needs to be a careful study, or series of studies, to determine the number of children who really need residential care. Criteria need to be developed for the use of institutional treatment and community-based care. Incentives need to be developed to encourage private, not-for-profit agencies to restructure themselves. They should be encouraged to divest themselves of some of their residential treatment capabilities in favor of developing other less costly and less intrusive options. Incentives also need to be developed to improve the quality and effectiveness of residential care because there will always be children needing housing in such facilities.

There also needs to be an immediate and careful examination of all abuse and neglect cases currently in residential treatment. Individual case plans should be developed to: (1) substantially reduce the time these youth are kept in treatment; and (2) insure, to the extent possible, that these youth are moved as quickly as possible into permanent placements and provided with appropriate aftercare and transition services to increase the chances for making the permanent placements successful. Our research indicates that older, male, and handicapped children should be given special attention as they are more likely to move into institutional care. In our study, it appears that handicapped status often means that the child has some kind of disability that interferes with learning. This means that strategies designed to reduce the number of children in institutional care must include services to address these special education needs.

The problems surrounding child caring institutions in Michigan are not unique to that state. Virtually every state has a large component of institutional care. The best available evidence suggests that outcomes from these types of interventions are both costly and questionable (Schwartz, 1994). There is little doubt that some children have to be managed in a twenty-four-hour, well-staffed and programmatically self-contained setting. Children needing such services should not be denied access to the treatment they need. However, if such treatment is to be provided, we must make sure it is provided to those who absolutely need it. We must also be willing to invest in high quality aftercare and transition services and semi-independent and independent living arrangements. This will help insure that educational and treatment gains made during a child's residential experience are maintained and built upon when they are returned to the community.

In addition, the federal government must develop an aggressive effort to inform and educate child welfare administrators, state and local elected public officials, child advocates, the media, and professional associations as to what is known about child care institutions, their effectiveness and what role they should play in a twenty-first century child welfare system. Child welfare administrators and policymakers in the states should also carefully examine the costs and benefits of the child care institutions in their child welfare systems. If they find results similar to our findings in Michigan, they should make a concerted attempt to reform and restructure this component of their system.

There is much support nationally for "de-categorizing" funds and giving child welfare administrators more flexibility to use resources to meet the needs of children and families. While this idea has merit, more flexibility in the hands of officials in jurisdictions where they might be inclined to use more costly and ineffective service options and where officials may be easily manipulated by political pressure to maintain the status quo will only exacerbate an already deeply rooted problem. Restricting funds for specific purposes, or categorization, was originally designed to insure that resources were used for specific purposes. While this idea seems no longer to be in vogue in child welfare, broad discretion regarding how funds are used may contribute to more problems than might be solved. Efforts to increase discretion should not eliminate safeguards against the overuse of institutional care and the development of incentives to promote permanency for all children regardless of whether they are in an institution or some other kind of out-of-home care.

Whatever child welfare reform strategies are implemented to both limit the use of and improve the quality and effectiveness of institutional care should draw upon the best available research. They should also be carefully studied in order to improve management and treatment intervention decisions. Any plan to reduce institutional placements should include collecting data on all children who are placed in institutions in order to see how long they are in such care, to find out whether they eventually move to a permanent home, and to explore whether alternative and less costly services can adequately meet their needs.

REFERENCES

Caldwell, D. W. (1993, May 10). *Memorandum to county directors and district office managers regarding the county performance report for the quarter ending December 1992*. Lansing: Michigan Department of Social Services.

Durkin, R. P., and Durkin, A. B. (1975). Evaluating residential treatment programs for disturbed children. In M. Guttentag and M. Struening (Eds.), *Handbook of evaluation research* (vol. 2). Beverly Hills, CA: Sage.

Edwards, J. K. (1994). Children in residential treatment: How many, What kind? Do we really know? *Residential Treatment for Children & Youth, 12*(1), 85–99.

Kresnak, J. (1993, May 28). Must kids pay to save families? *Detroit Free Press*, p. A1.

Michigan Department of Social Services (MDSS). (1992, February 25). *Testimony on Children's Services before the Michigan House Appropriations Subcommittee on Social Services.* National Institute of Mental Health. (August, 1983). *Residential treatment, centers for emotionally disturbed children 1977–78 and 1979–80. (Statistical Note 162).* Rockville, MD: Division of Biometry and Epidemiology, Survey and Reports Branch.

Papenfort, D.; Young, T.; and Dore, M. (1988). Residential group care for children considered emotionally disturbed: 1966–1981. *Social Service Review, 62*(1), 158–70.

Schwartz, I .M. (1994). Child caring institutions: The "Edsels" of children's services. In E. Gambrill and T. Stein (Eds.), *Controversial issues in social work.* Boston: Allyn and Bacon.

Tatara, T. (1993). *Characteristics of children in substitute and adoptive care.* Washington, DC: American Public Welfare Association.

Wells, K. (1991). Long-term residential treatment for children: Introduction. *American Orthopsychiatric Association, 61*(3), 324–26.

CHAPTER 7

Public Policy and Child Welfare: Agenda for the 21st Century

The history of child welfare is littered with well-intentioned but largely failed reform efforts. Despite the billions in federal, state, and local dollars poured into child welfare systems annually, media scandals and class action lawsuits, state and federal inquiries into child welfare services, the recommendations of national standard-setting organizations, and the efforts of private foundations and child advocacy groups, no state or county has been recognized for having a model system.

Child welfare systems have insatiable appetites. They can absorb almost any amount of money thrown at them by federal and state elected public officials, particularly those being pressured to do something about child maltreatment complaints or class action lawsuits stemming from abusive and unprofessional practices. Hagedorn, a respected academic who took time off from the ivory tower to join a team charged with reforming the infamous child welfare system in Milwaukee, believes that public child welfare systems are pernicious because of the way they manage to thrive, even in a difficult fiscal environment when other services are being cut back. He also thinks the administrators of some of these agencies have become adept at getting their way. For example, they will often scare politicians by implying that children may die or there may be scandals and lawsuits if they don't get more money for more child protective service and foster care workers. Hagedorn feels these tactics have improved the job market for child welfare workers and expanded child welfare bureaucracies, but have had little impact on improving the quality and effectiveness of services to abused and neglected children (Hagedorn, 1995).

Although this is a discouraging picture, we cannot give up. We must keep trying to develop new and more effective strategies for reform. The traditional approaches have not served us well, and they are not likely to serve us well in the future. Also, as we contemplate the kinds of initiatives needed to reform child welfare, we should be mindful of the words of the National Commission on Children. As we pointed out in the first chapter, after surveying the child welfare landscape, the commission concluded that radical reforms are needed and that tinkering at the margins of the system won't accomplish much. Unfortunately, when it came time to making recommendations the commission failed to heed its own warning. The commission's recommendations were far from radical, with some being ill conceived and not even based upon the best available research. This is because the commission turned to the child welfare establishment in the United States for answers, the establishment that is heavily vested in maintaining the status quo. So, where do we go from here? The rest of this chapter tries to address this tough question.

ATTACKING CHILD ABUSE BY ELIMINATING POVERTY

Many respected scholars, social policy experts, child welfare professionals, and child advocates do not believe that much progress will be made toward preventing child abuse and neglect until we tackle the issue of poverty, particularly child poverty. Lindsey (1994) reminds us that "child abuse is not the major reason children are removed from their parents. Rather, inadequacy of income, more than any other factor, constitutes the reason that children are removed" (p. 155). Research by Van Voorhis and Gilbert indicates that "child fatality rates are strongly correlated with rates of children in poverty, but barely affected by child abuse reporting system performance measures (Van Voorhis and Gilbert, *Children and Youth Services Review*, Vol. 20, Number 3, 1998, p. 219)." Their research "underline the crucial role of broader environmental factors and the limits to which performance measures such as reporting and out-of-home placement rates are associated with protecting children from the most severe harm (Ibid)."

We also believe there will not be any major advancements in preventing and ameliorating child abuse and neglect until more progress is made in eradicating poverty. However, as we pointed out in chapter 1, the relationship between poverty and child maltreatment is complex and there is still much about the relationship that we do not fully understand. For example, the current and unprecedented economic success in the United States does not seem to be impacting the people at the very bottom of the economic ladder. Moreover, the disparity between this socioeconomic group and other groups is increasing. There are also serious questions about whether the economic boom and the welfare reforms being implemented will ever have a major impact on improving the economic and social conditions of this population. Although we'll probably know a lot more about this in the future, the preliminary data, as limited as it is, is not particularly encouraging. As of now, it does not appear that the "rising tide" is raising all boats.

Politicians are crediting the large drop in the welfare rolls to welfare reform. Others are crediting the growth in the economy. The decline is probably due to both, with most experts attributing the bulk of the drop to economic factors. We don't have a clear picture about what impact, if any, the large drop in the welfare rolls has had on child maltreatment. We do know that the numbers of children being removed from their homes because of abuse and neglect is still increasing, although there are signs that the rates of out-of-home placement may be leveling off. Also, most of the children being taken away from their parents are being removed because of neglect. These issues raise many important questions. For example, why hasn't the economic boom in the United States had an impact on curbing placements into the child welfare system? What is the prognosis for the future? Will eliminating poverty for those at the very bottom of the socioeconomic ladder prevent all types of child maltreatment? Or, will it have differential effects depending on the type of child maltreatment? In other words, will eliminating poverty among this group result in significant reductions in the incidence of child neglect or will it have just as much of an impact on child physical and sexual abuse? Will the decline in the welfare rolls be permanent or will they increase the future? What will happen to the children of the poor when their parents are no longer eligible to receive welfare benefits? Remember, one of the major changes in the welfare system is that families, including children, will only be eligible for cash assistance for a specified period of time. This happened when Congress and the Clinton administration eliminated the politically unpopular AFDC program and replaced with the Temporary Assistance to Needy Families program, or TANF.

There are many who believe the child welfare system will swell when impoverished adults are no longer eligible for cash assistance, particularly if they aren't earning enough to support themselves and their children or are unemployed. Although the supporters of the recent welfare reform measures believe that welfare recipients dropped from the rolls will get jobs, preliminary data from New York raises serious questions about whether this will in fact be the case (*New York Times*, March 23, 1998, p. 1). There are also questions about whether new or restructured welfare-to-work programs will have a major impact on those at the bottom of the socioeconomic ladder. Again, only time will tell. The general feeling is that the welfare recipients who have benefited the most from the booming economy and welfare-to-work programs thus far were a much less troubled population than those that remain on welfare. This, many experts suggest, made it relatively easy to move them into the workforce; something these same experts believe will be considerably more difficult for those still on the welfare rolls.

Lindsey (1994) has proposed the creation of something like a social security system for children as a long-term strategy for attacking child poverty. Lindsey suggests that funds be invested in a Children's Trust Fund where the principal could grow through expert management and additional contributions. The funds would be available to the beneficiaries, older needy children to help them make the transition from childhood to adulthood. The funds could only be used for "approved" purposes (e.g., employment training, college tuition, etc.). The beneficiaries would be required to repay the benefits they received, possibly including interest, from the wages they earned later in adulthood (pp. 312–13). This, Lindsey suggests, would help insure that poor children would have the assets needed to become productive citizens in a 21st century free market economy and prevent their children from being born into and having to grow up in poverty. Lindsey (1994) also advocates a Universal Child Support Collection System. Plotnick (1997) also believes that child poverty can be significantly reduced, but he has suggested some other approaches. He contends that

Policies (designed) to raise employment and earnings do work, but at their current size and intensity the increased earnings they produce have only a small impact on child poverty. If their scope and intensity were expanded aggressively, further earnings increases might result. Such efforts may need to be accompanied with expanded public outlays on child care for single-parent families to realize their potential" (pp. 84–85).

Plotnick (1997) also thinks that a refundable child tax credit and large-scale public service employment programs could make a difference. Others point to the benefits of the Earned Income Tax Credit for low income wage earners as an effective strategy for helping families to make ends meet.

While there is no shortage of ideas about how to address the problem of child poverty, the chances that the Clinton administration and the Congress will be receptive to any of them at this time, particularly if they will be costly, are zero. They are too enthralled with the welfare reform initiatives recently put into place and with the unprecedented nationwide drop in the welfare rolls. Also, despite the fact that the preliminary data is less than encouraging with respect to those at the very bottom of the socioeconomic ladder, it is too early to tell what the ultimate impact of the changes in the welfare system will be. As we said earlier, only time will tell. There are a number of other domestic issues that politicians consider to be of much higher priority than child poverty. For example, President Clinton has already announced his plans to focus attention on making Medicare and Social Security solvent for the baby boomer generation. The President also wants to significantly expand the availability of child care, particularly to welfare recipients who desperately need affordable child care if their children are to be properly cared for while they are in job training programs or are employed.

The idea of eliminating child poverty might seem like a fantasy or a pipe dream. However, we would like to point out that the nation committed itself to eliminating poverty among the elderly back in the 1960s, and this important goal has largely been achieved. Our nation's children, who are our future, deserve no less.

While we strongly support the goal of eliminating child poverty, the reality is that this will require a long-term national commitment and will take decades to achieve. Moreover, as desirable as this may be, there is no consensus of public and political opinion that the elimination of child poverty be adopted as a national goal. This would have to occur before any meaningful strategy could be implemented. There are also serious questions about whether child poverty can be eliminated without providing benefits to their primary caregivers, who are single mothers. This is not a group that enjoys broad public and political support. Lindsey's call for the establishment of a Children's Trust Fund, or social security system for children, may prove to an effective strategy for getting around this dilemma. However, more details about Lindsey's proposal need to be flushed out before it could ever be given serious consideration. Moreover, there are serious concerns that the federal welfare reform legislation signed by President Clinton will exacerbate the child poverty problem by creating more of it (Moynihan, 1996).

Also, as difficult and challenging as the elimination of poverty among the elderly was, this was not nearly as formidable as the elimination of child poverty would be. To begin with, elderly citizens who are poor are viewed very differently than other groups in similar circumstances. Impoverished elderly citizens are considered to be the "deserving poor." Others who are poor, including children, are considered to be the "undeserving poor." The elderly also constitute a large and growing political force which politicians have to heed and respond to. President Clinton's proposal to target budget surplus funds to keep social security solvent is a case in point. In addition, taking care of the elderly is an enormously popular issue among the American middle class. It appeals to the middle class, who are also a large and influential political force in the country, because it means that the government will provide significant economic and health benefits to their parents in the form of entitlements. If this were not the case, children of the elderly would be forced to pay for the care themselves.

In other words, the universal nature and egalitarian approach to treating the elderly stems from the fact that it does not just impact the parents of the poor. In contrast, the parents of poor children, particularly minorities, have a very poor record of participating in the political process and, as a result, have little or no influence on important national and state public policy. They are unable to put the issue of poverty in general, and child poverty in particular, on the public agenda. Also, impoverished children, however deplorable their situation may be, have not captured the attention and concern of the broader society. The one exception is health where there does appear to be universal support for insuring that all children, including poor children, have access to the health care they need. The reality is that until the more fortunate and relatively affluent classes in the United States come to feel that they have a personal stake in the eradication of poverty, or even child poverty, it is unlikely to happen.

Poverty isn't the only issue that needs to be tackled if significant inroads are going to be made in preventing child maltreatment. There is a significant shortage of affordable housing in the United States. Strategies must be implemented to prevent the existing affordable housing stock from deteriorating and, at the same time, stimulate the construction of new affordable housing, particularly in our large cities. There is also some data suggesting that parental characteristics associated with higher earnings are more closely related with improved child outcomes than is the case simply with unearned income (Susan Mayer, *What Money Can't Buy*, Harvard University Press, p. 230). While the data are far from compelling, this is an issue that certainly warrants closer examination.

It has been estimated that 40 million people in the United States are not covered by health care of any form. Many of these individuals are children. It is inconceivable to envision a strategy designed significantly to reduce child maltreatment that does not include universal access to health care or, at the very least, universal health coverage for children. Much progress has already been made on the health care front, and more will probably be made in the years ahead. Because of the broad public support for health care, the chances for progress in this area are greater than for the others mentioned above.

While these broader social issues need to be addressed before we can expect to see any major progress in attacking the root causes of child maltreatment, we cannot lose sight of the fact that the child welfare system is in a state of crisis. This is why some are calling for a return to orphanages as a strategy for coping with the large and growing numbers of children being taken away from their parents. We must act immediately to fully protect and properly care for the half million children in our public child welfare systems, many of whom are at risk while in the custody of state and local governments. We cannot afford to wait until the electorate and our elected public officials decide to attack the problems of poverty, inadequate health care, and the lack of affordable housing before taking action.

CURRENT REFORM INITIATIVES AT THE FEDERAL AND STATE LEVELS

Policymakers at the federal and state levels are well aware of the crisis in child welfare and are taking steps to try to address the situation. As we mentioned in chapter 3, President Clinton made additional federal funds available to the states as an incentive to increase the number of adoptions. The president's goal is to double the number of public child welfare agency adoptions by the year 2002. Although this would be a step in the right direction, doubling the number of public agency adoptions would only increase them from an estimated 27,000 to 54,000; the best available data suggests that the number could easily be tripled or even quadrupled.

Legislation has also been passed in some states making it easier to remove children from dangerous home situations. Prompted by deaths of children from families well known to child welfare authorities and the backlash from ill-conceived family preservation policies and programs, these state laws mark the beginning of a watershed in child welfare by signaling that child protection and safety takes precedence over trying to keep abusive and neglectful families together or reunifying them.

The most visible and significant development, however, was the enactment of the Adoption and Safe Families Act of 1997 (P.L. 105–89) in November, 1997. This act is the most comprehensive and sweeping set of reforms enacted by Congress since the passage of the Adoption Assistance and Child Welfare Act of 1980 (P.L. 96–272). The 1997 act was carefully crafted to appeal to a broad range of vocal, politically active, and increasingly more ideologically diverse child welfare constituencies and special interest groups. It continues and increases the amount of financial support for family preservation and support programs, which will please the professional child welfare establishment, supporters of family preservation programs, and child advocacy groups such as the Child Welfare League of America and the Children's Defense Fund.

Unfortunately, Congress chose to overlook the fact that there isn't enough credible scientific evidence to make a compelling case for continuing to pour scarce resources into family preservation programs, let alone expanding them. At the very least, Congress should have waited until the results from a HHS funded national evaluation of family preservation programs became available before investing additional resources in them. It certainly would have been nice to see national child welfare policy driven by research for a change rather than ideology. What this points out is that family preservation programs are too popular to eliminate, scale down, or even try to restructure (e.g., require that they be targeted to prevent placements in costly residential treatment programs).

Like some of the laws previously enacted in the states, the1997 act places more emphasis on protecting children and makes it easier to remove them from dangerous home environments. The legislation calls for placing more of the burden on abusive and neglectful parents to demonstrate that they can properly care for their children before they will be returned to them. It also reduces the amount of time children have to stay in foster care from eighteen months to twelve months before permanent plans have to be made for them. Senator DeWine, one of the authors of the bill, pointed out that some of the provisions in the Act were designed to address the problems created by the "reasonable efforts" provisions in P.L. 96–272. DeWine remarked that P.L. 96–272 "has been misinterpreted in such a way that no matter what the particular circumstances of a household may be, it is argued that the State must make reasonable efforts to keep that family together and to put it back together if it falls apart" (Congressional Record, Nov. 13, 1997). He noted, as have others, that "reasonable efforts" has come to mean "unreasonable efforts" to try to keep abusive families together or reunite them.

Building on the course set by President Clinton, the 1997 act provides incentives to increase the number of adoptions and limits the amount of time children can be kept in foster care before states are required to terminate parental rights. For example, the act authorizes cash bonuses to be paid to states as an incentive to increase the number of adoptions. $4,000 will be paid for every foster child adopted and $6,000 for every child with special needs adopted. While there are some who feel these incentives are too small to make a significant difference, they represent an important step in the right direction. They certainly can be increased in the future if they prove to be inadequate. Equally important, the use of incentives, in this case fiscal incentives, is an indicator that elected public officials are looking to borrow concepts and strategies from the private sector for reforming child welfare in the United States. This is something that is long overdue and will probably have major implications for the future.

Some requirements of the act are set forth below:

in the case of a child who has been in foster care under the responsibility of the State for 15 of the most recent 22 months, or, if a court of competent jurisdiction has determined a child to be an abandoned infant (as defined under State law), made a determination that the parent has committed murder of another child of the parent, committed voluntary manslaughter of another child of the parent, aided or abetted, attempted, conspired, or solicited to commit such a murder or such a voluntary manslaughter, or committed a felony assault that has resulted in serious bodily injury to the child or another child of the parent, the State shall file a petition to terminate the parental rights of the child's parents (or, if such a petition has been filed by another party, seek to be joined as a party to the petition), and, concurrently, to identify, recruit, process, and approve a qualified family for an adoption,

unless "emphasis added"

"(i)" at the option of the State, the child is being cared for by a relative;

"(ii)" a State agency has documented in the case plan (which shall be available for court review) a compelling reason for determining that filing such a petition would not be in the best interests of the child; or

"(iii)" the State has not provided to the family of the child, consistent with the time period in the State case plan, such services as the State deems necessary for the safe return of the child to the child's home, if reasonable efforts of the type described in section 471(a)(15)(ii) are required to be made with respect to the child." (H.R. 867)

While the Adoption and Safe Families Act of 1997 encourages states to give more priority to insuring the health and safety of children and restricts the time children can be held in foster care until permanent plans are made for them, it doesn't go far enough. For example, the act doesn't contain time limits within which states must comply with its provisions. Also, with its continued emphasis on family preservation programs, the act sends a mixed message that could become problematic as the legislation is implemented. While there is reason to be optimistic about the act, the mandates in the law are far from radical and not nearly as bold as the National Commission on Children believed were necessary to overhaul the child welfare system.

There are also some loopholes in the act that could severely limit its impact. For example, the stipulations preceded by *"unless"* in the excerpt above are worrisome. Moreover, some child welfare officials and juvenile court judges are already complaining that the crafters of the legislation have failed to take into account how the system really operates. They note that it may take months just to schedule court hearings on child welfare cases which makes the time frames for processing cases unrealistic. In any event, Congress and other watchdog groups will have to be vigilant and monitor the impact of these provisions very carefully or little will be accomplished. It is also important to keep in mind that the act does not address the issue of poverty. Because of this, it is doubtful that it will stem the tide of children being propelled into the child welfare system to begin with.

There is also another and more subtle issue that needs to be watched: "transinstitutionalization," a term coined by Paul Lerman. Transinstitutionalization is the transfer or movement of children from one system of social control (e.g., juvenile justice, child welfare, mental health) to another (Lerman, 1980). Lerman studied the historical patterns and trends regarding the institutionalization of children in the United States. He concluded that the overall rates of confinement or placement of children in the juvenile justice, child welfare and children's mental health systems remained relatively constant over time. However, the rates of confinement or placement within these systems changed dramatically. In other words, if the rates of confinement in the juvenile justice system declined significantly, they tended to be offset by corresponding increases in the child welfare, and/or mental health systems. If the rates of placement declined in the child welfare system, they were offset by increases in the juvenile justice and/or mental health systems.

Lerman attributed the movement of children among these systems to the fact that the boundaries them were far more porous than people thought. He also observed that a large number of the children who came to the attention of official authorities did so because they were "troubled" and exhibited various kinds of "acting out" behaviors, behaviors or problems that would qualify them for admission into more than one of these systems of social control. Other factors that contributed to this phenomenon included transferring legal responsibility for children, funding incentives and disincentives, and the growth of facilities in a given sector or sectors.

Lerman's work suggests that it is conceivable that reforms implemented under the Adoption and Safe Families Act that would precipitate significant declines in the child welfare population might well be offset by increases in the juvenile justice and/or mental health systems. Obviously, older children (ten years of age and older) who might be diverted or removed from the child welfare system would be particularly vulnerable to this. In light of this, elected public officials and program administrators should take preventive steps to make sure that children are not shuffled from one system of social control to another under the guise of "reform." Also, child advocates and researchers should be vigilant about observing whether this begins to happen and, if so, developing solutions to the problem before it becomes widespread.

In the final analysis, the states will be responsible for implementing the Adoption and Safe Families of 1997. States will have a lot of discretion in determining how they will meet the provisions in the act, substantively and in spirit. While history suggests we should be very modest in our expectations, the act could be used as a major instrument for reform. Because of this, governors, state legislators, public interest groups, child advocates, and practitioners should view this legislation as presenting an opportunity for real change.

OTHER PROMISING STRATEGIES

The federal and state initiatives described above, if properly administered, could have a constructive impact on child welfare services all across the country. Other policy and program initiatives that could help to reform child welfare are discussed below.

Developing a Model System

About fifteen years ago the General Motors Company (GM) announced plans to locate a site to build their new Saturn automobile. In making the announcement, GM officials indicated that they would entertain proposals from individual states. The prospect of winning this economic prize had every governor salivating. At stake were thousands of new jobs and an enhanced ability to attract many other new businesses. Governors across the country responded to the challenge by launching campaigns to persuade GM to select their state. Governors pulled together teams of key elected and appointed public officials, private sector representatives, university officials, and civic leaders to come up with reasons, programs, and incentives for convincing GM officials that their state was best suited for the Saturn project. In the end, GM selected the state of Tennessee. One of the key factors tilting the scale in Tennessee's favor was a long-term commitment by elected public officials to improve the state's public education system. This commitment was designed to insure a well-trained labor force for GM and other companies far into the future.

The process generated an extraordinary amount of activity and creative thinking in the states about how best to meet this challenge. It served as a catalyst for mobilizing some of the best brainpower and leadership to focus on the issue. The proposals that were developed had the political and other kinds of support needed to help make them a reality.

If nothing else, the process demonstrated just how energetic, creative, and responsive elected public officials and others in the states could be when the stakes were high and the potential payoff was great. We think something similar is needed in child welfare. Child welfare systems are an embarrassment in practically every state and local jurisdiction and a thorn in the side of governors and local officials.

The federal administration, perhaps in collaboration with private foundations, should set aside a substantial amount of money and award funds on a competitive and relatively long-term basis as incentives to a small, but carefully selected, number of states, counties, and cities that develop innovative and, to the extent possible, data-driven and research-based plans to overhaul their child welfare systems. The administration might also consider granting waivers with few or no strings attached to states, allowing them to utilize the federal funds they receive under the Adoption and Safe Families Act of 1997 to develop the most creative and bold plans for restructuring their systems and more effectively addressing the needs of children and families.   The possibilities for real reform could be strengthened by encouraging states to develop strategies designed to attack poverty so we could actually test whether this would make the difference many think it would. If this were done, it might even be more attractive to the foundation community and could also yield valuable data and information that could guide poverty policies in the future.

Child welfare systems are creatures of the state.   If real and lasting reforms in child welfare are going to be realized, they will have to be initiated from within the states themselves and have the state and local level political and public support needed to bring them about and to sustain them. Governors, county executives, and mayors should be encouraged to reach out and involve their legislatures, representatives from the business community, civic leaders, the media, child welfare professionals, health and mental health professionals, local elected officials, and universities. While the process should be designed to encourage creative thinking and bold new approaches with a minimum of federal bureaucratic interference and regulation, the plans should clearly indicate how the most difficult and challenging problems confronting state and local child welfare systems will be addressed.

Universities can be particularly helpful in examining child welfare data for use in understanding how child welfare systems really operate, identifying key issues needing to be addressed, and making informed policy recommendations. Universities can also help by evaluating the impact of reforms. The federal government can assist by providing technical expertise and information about resources that states and localities can take advantage of during the planning process.   It is hoped that this will result in a few jurisdictions emerging as models for the rest of the nation.

Conceivably, this strategy might generate ideas and proposals for dismantling existing child welfare system bureaucracies in favor of new, more exciting, more flexible, more humane, and more comprehensive service delivery systems. In fact, we hope this approach will liberate state and local officials to be creative and not be constrained by existing bureaucratic structures and programs. As stated earlier, this strategy could also include testing ideas designed to eradicate poverty, particularly child poverty. It could also lead to more innovative and effective approaches involving the private not-for-profit and for-profit sectors in designing, managing, and delivering services as well. It could also lead to the development of real competition in the delivery of child welfare services and the use of meaningful incentives for encouraging and rewarding performance.

Limiting the Mission of the Child Welfare System

The current mission of the child welfare system is to both protect children and preserve families. It does neither of these things very well. It took on the role of preserving families in the early 1980s, largely in response to the mushrooming family preservation movement. At the time the child welfare system assumed this major new responsibility, it was already failing in its basic mission of protecting children. This is something the advocates of family preservation (e.g., the child welfare establishment, child advocacy organizations, and staff from a few influential private foundations) chose to overlook. They also saw no conflict between the goals of protecting children while, at the same time, trying to keep them at home or reuniting them with their abusive and neglectful parents. However, in reality, these two policy thrusts have often proved to be fundamentally incompatible and a source of confusion on the part of child welfare workers. As Gelles has noted, "That the child welfare system is asked to both investigate families and help families is the enduring paradox of the system" (Gelles, 1996, p. 157).

In fairness, policymakers and practitioners found family preservation to be an easy policy to embrace. It is consistent with the deeply held belief in the sacredness of the family unit and that families should not be interfered with by the government. It was also based on the assumption, or myth, that a bad home situation was a better environment than, perhaps, the best foster home or other type of out-of-home placement.

We should abandon the dual mission of the child welfare system and limit it to protecting children and insuring their safety (Gelles, 1996, Lindsey, 1994). Vulnerable and mistreated children should be allowed to remain in their own homes or be returned to their birth parents only if their safety can be guaranteed. While services should be made available to parents who abuse and neglect their children and their children should be returned to them if they can demonstrate that they can care for them properly, this goal should be secondary to that of insuring that children are protected and receive the care and nurturing they need. Moreover, we should not keep children in foster care for years until they are provided with permanent placements, including adoption. This, in part, is what the Adoption and Safe Families Act is designed to address.

Restructure and Redeploy Family Preservation Resources and Services

States should redeploy some of their family preservation resources toward preventing placements in costly group homes residential treatment centers, and inpatient psychiatric and substance abuse facilities. These resources are now largely being used to prevent the placement of abused and neglected children in family foster care. From a policy perspective, there simply isn't enough credible evidence to make a compelling argument that family preservation services used for this purpose are effective (see chap. 2). There is, however, evidence that family preservation services are effective in preventing placements in costly group, residential treatment, and in-patient psychiatric and substance abuse programs.

In other words, family preservation resources targeted exclusively toward preventing placements in foster care are being squandered. While children and families may be receiving services they need and want and these services may be helpful to troubled families in many ways, family preservation programs are not having the impact that many had hoped for.

Defining Child Abuse as a Crime and Investigating Child Abuse Complaints

Leroy Pelton (1992) is one of the leading advocates for separating the child abuse investigative function from the rest of child welfare services (e.g., foster care, case management, family preservation services, adoptions, and reunification services). Richard Gelles (1996) and Duncan Lindsey (1994) have now weighed in on this issue and have made similar recommendations. These respected scholars and students of child welfare maintain that professional social workers are not trained to do this kind of work. Instead, they recommend that the task of investigating child abuse and neglect complaints be carried out by trained investigators.

Lindsey (1994) also feels that the "Responsibility for receiving, investigating, and prosecuting cases of severe child abuse requires coercive intervention and needs to be clearly assigned to the police" (p. 9). He argues that "Child abuse, in whatever degree, is criminal assault and needs to be recognized as such. It requires firm investigation and prosecution by the police, backed by the courts" (p. 169). He also notes that "There is no evidence that the transformation of the child welfare system into protective services has resulted in reduced child abuse fatalities. Nor is their evidence that children are safer as a result of the transformation" (p. 125).

We, too, think the time has come to separate the child protective service investigative function from the rest of child welfare services. We also believe that child physical and sexual abuse should be treated as crimes and the perpetrators, including parents, should be prosecuted to the fullest extent of the law. Spousal abuse is a crime in the United States. If beating and sexually assaulting a spouse are considered violent criminal acts, why shouldn't the same behavior perpetrated against children be viewed in the same way? Also, given the trend in the United States toward prosecuting and sentencing juveniles, including young children, as adults for committing violent crimes, it is hard to justify excusing the same behavior on the part of adults just because their victims happen to be their own children.

The criminal statutes in states include definitions of violent crimes that would encompass behavior such as child physical and sexual abuse. Any modifications that might be needed in state laws that are already on the books are likely to be minor.

Severe neglect should also be considered a crime. However, the threshold and definition of what might constitute severe neglect is not always clear. In this case, legislatures will have to grapple with this issue and develop criteria for what constitutes criminal neglect of children.

Congressional Oversight and Review of Child Welfare

Congress should carefully monitor the implementation of the Adoption and Safe Families Act of 1997 on a regular basis. This should include assessing the impact of the act, considering relevant research findings that would have major policy and program implications, and making adjustments in the legislation as needed. Frankly, given the sorry state of child welfare nationally (refer to chap. 1) it would be very surprising if the mandates in the new federal act were implemented effectively. There has never been a comprehensive and objective review of the Adoption Assistance and Child Welfare Act of 1980, and we hope it will not take another seventeen years before Congress will do something significant in this area.

In addition, Congress should carefully and systematically examine the problems confronting the child welfare system in the United States and reevaluate the role the federal government is playing in this critical area. The number of children being taken away from their parents by state and local child welfare officials and being placed into foster care is increasing. Moreover, child advocates, child welfare professionals, and academics are predicting that the numbers may continue to grow well into the foreseeable future. Equally troubling is the fact that federal child welfare expenditures have been increasing at an alarming rate. This is not what Congress envisioned when it passed the Adoption Assistance and Child Welfare Act of 1980 (and the subsequent reauthorizations of this legislation), the Family Preservation and Support Act of 1993, and, most recently, the Adoption and Safe Families Act of 1997. In conducting this review, Congress should address such questions as:

What really accounts for the growth in the numbers of children in foster care and what, realistically, needs to be done about it? What impact will the Adoption and Safe Families Act of 1997 have on this problem?

Why are so many public child welfare systems vulnerable to litigation and what has been accomplished as a result of these lawsuits?

What role should the federal government play in child welfare in the future?

Should federal policy continue to encourage state and local child welfare systems to both preserve families and protect children?

What role, if any, should the federal government play in encouraging states to treat child abuse as a crime?

What steps need to be taken to insure that children placed into the custody of public child welfare agencies receive the finest care possible?

What additional reforms need to be implemented to increase the number of adoptions?

What are the advantages and disadvantages of privatizing child welfare services?

What role should managed care play in child welfare and what can be learned from the experiences in the health care field? Also, what are the experiences in states that are already applying managed care principles to child welfare?

In addition, Congress and the administration should consider developing an effective strategy for controlling costs. At the present time, there is no cap on appropriations for foster care. With the exception of the fiscal match required by states, there are no real incentives for controlling costs at the federal, state, and local levels. Perhaps it is time for Congress and the administration to consider creating incentives, in addition to those recently developed for adoptions, and disincentives that would strongly encourage states to place children in permanent and safe environments as quickly as possible. Perhaps, as is now the case with welfare, Congress and the administration should consider capping and block-granting federal child welfare funds and giving states more flexibility in determining how those resources can be used. Another option would be for the federal government to pay for the full cost of foster care for each child for a specified period of time and nothing thereafter. If states choose or need to keep children in foster care beyond that period of time, perhaps they should pay for the cost of such care entirely from state revenues. There are also no incentives or disincentives to encourage public child welfare agencies to make permanent placements that endure. If there were, it might cut down on the relatively high rates of return to foster care.

Managed Care and the For-Profit Privatization of the Management and Delivery of Child Welfare Services

Historically, federal child welfare funds could only be used by public agencies and nonprofit organizations. In 1997, Congress opened the door to allow these funds to be used by for-profit organizations. Child advocates and the professional child welfare establishment claim this was done in secrecy and without their knowledge (Bernstein, 1997). The implication here is that they would have lobbied against this because for-profit organizations, particularly the large health care conglomerates eyeing the child welfare system as a significant new market of opportunity, are only interested in profits. Critics of this move are concerned that greed and return on investments for shareholders will result in substandard and abusive services to abused and neglected children.

The concerns being raised about for-profits entering the child welfare field are real. The health care field is rife with fraud, greed, and questionable management and health care service delivery practices. There are mounting complaints from consumers about shoddy practices, poor quality of services, denial of needed care, excessive bureaucratic procedures, and indifference toward patients and their needs. These problems, if transferred to the child welfare system, would be disastrous. In fact, if one wants to see some of the negative aspects of for-profit takeover of the management and delivery of services to children and youth, one need only look at the developments in the juvenile justice field. While there are some success stories, there are numerous examples of profit-making organizations running youth correctional programs that are as bad or worse than programs operated by the public and not-for-profit sectors. There are also examples of contracts with for-profit companies having to be cancelled because of incompetence, mismanagement, and abusive and unprofessional practices.

Although the movement of for-profit companies into the child welfare marketplace could have adverse implications, we don't think this will make matters any worse than they already are. In fact, we think there is much to gain from their involvement in the field. The reality is that the professional child welfare establishment hasn't done a good job. As we pointed out in chapter 1, the public child welfare systems in more than half the states are either under federal court order or some type of court-approved settlement agreement or in the advanced stages of litigation because their systems are abusive and substandard. Many of them cannot even guarantee the health and safety of the children in their custody. The same is true for dozens of county and city operated child welfare systems. These systems are well known for being mismanaged, wasteful, inefficient, and indifferent toward the children and families they serve.

We also believe that competition in the child welfare "marketplace" is long overdue and would be a constructive development in the field. We believe that elected public officials would be well advised to explore the potential benefits from privatizing their public child welfare systems and the ways this could be done responsibly. One possibility would be to experiment with privatization in one or two regions of a state or locality and compare the results with the traditional way in which services are delivered. Another strategy would be to privatize parts of the system. Not all for-profit health care groups are only concerned about profits, particularly at the expense of their patients. Some are concerned with providing high quality services and meeting the highest professional standards while keeping costs to a minimum. Some of these health care organizations have already hired some of the better public and private child welfare agency administrators in the country to oversee and manage their work in child welfare. These professionals will help to insure that the services their companies are contracted to deliver will be effective and will meet the highest professional standards.   Hopefully, they won't be corrupted by the lure of big salaries and profits.

In addition, the private sector brings efficient and effective management and business practices, information technology, experience with managed care, and an orientation toward outcomes and performance that can only help the child welfare field. Also, the entry of the for-profit sector into the child welfare field will put the existing child welfare system on notice, and one can hope that the competition for business and contracts will improve the quality of services across the board. In fact, this is already beginning to occur. For profit health care groups have been contracted with to manage or deliver public child welfare services in Kansas, Ohio, and Pennsylvania. Officials in other states are also exploring this option. These developments are creating a stir within the existing child welfare establishment and causing more attention to be focused on outcomes, performance indicators, and improving the quality of existing services. In some other jurisdictions policy makers are uneasy about opening up the competition for the management and delivery of child welfare services to for profit organizations. In these instances, such as in New York City, and in the state of Florida, officials are restricting the competition to existing and new non-profit providers, church groups and similar child care organizations. While we understand the concerns of these policymakers, we believe the imposition of tough quality of care standards coupled with tough and independent monitoring can minimize the dangers some see in for profit privatization.

Kansas was one of the first states to privatize its child welfare system. While the jury is still out on this development, a recent article that appeared in The Children's Vanguard reports some promising results after the first year of implementation. In most instances, the outcome and performance measures initially established were met or exceeded (*The Children's Vanguard*, February, 1998, pp. 6–11). For those interested in exploring the privatization option, the Kansas experience offers some important lessons and, especially, that the process can be transparent carefully and openly observed. This does not mean that the Kansas approach should be adopted by everyone or be viewed as a panacea.   It does represent, however, a strategy that is promising.   Each jurisdiction that adopts such a strategy would need to customize it to fit it own unique needs and goals.

Managed care models and concepts are also beginning to permeate the child welfare field. In fact, there is so much interest in this concept and it is spreading so fast that the Child Welfare League of America has created a Managed Care Institute dedicated to monitoring and tracking these developments and providing consultation and technical assistance in the area. The institute reports that more than forty states are actively looking into the possibilities that managed care offers. There are early indications that a variety of approaches to managed care in child welfare are in the process of being implemented. Some involve the for-profit sector, some are centered around the reorganization of non-profits into managed care entities or consortiums, and some involve a combination of the two. As is the case of the health care field, managed care could increase efficiency and control costs. Managed care could also be an important mechanism for bringing about much needed system reform and change in child welfare. It could, for example, open up entrepreneurial opportunities for the many creative and capable social workers now working in highly bureaucratic and ineffective systems. However, as stated earlier, there is also the possibility that managed care could focus undue attention on profits at the expense of quality of services. To avoid such danger, proper quality control and monitoring need to be established to insure that the safety and well being of children remains the main priority.

Information Technology

Much has been written about the sorry state of child welfare data, and we have dealt with this problem in earlier chapters. We also agree with those who have commented on the need to develop comprehensive and reliable child welfare management and service intervention information systems. In fact, officials in many states, counties, and cities are working to develop information systems to address these data deficiencies.

We think, however, that it is important to move beyond these developments. In particular, there is a critical need to explore how advancements in technology can help both improve and, more importantly, revolutionize how services are delivered. For example, a national adoptions agency based in Philadelphia is using the internet to make prospective adoptive parents aware of children legally free for adoption. Perhaps the preliminary screening of prospective adoptive families and conducting of home studies could be done with the help of technology as well. Child welfare workers could communicate with foster families and children in the child welfare system electronically and vice versa. Foster parent training could be conducted through distance learning. Also, public agencies could communicate more regularly and more efficiently with service providers and the children they are serving. While this will not eliminate the need for well-trained professional staff, taking advantage of existing technology could have a significant impact on restructuring how services are delivered.

Child Welfare Research

The federal government needs to play a greater role in encouraging and funding child welfare research. There is a desperate need to increase our knowledge about promising child welfare policies, practices, and direct service interventions. One of the consistent criticisms about child welfare is the lack of data available for effective planning and policy development. While this is certainly the case, and better information systems need to be developed, we think there is ample evidence from research in Illinois, California, New York,

Texas, and Michigan to believe that there is great untapped potential in existing state and local child welfare information systems. In the short run, therefore, the federal government should encourage states, particularly in collaboration with universities, to explore how existing data sets can be better utilized. If such collaborations were to take place with schools of social work, it could lead to the development of more relevant child welfare curricula, better trained professional social workers, and a more effective use of federal child welfare training funds.

In addition, the federal government should encourage states to make their child welfare data available to universities and child welfare researchers and provide resources to help bring this about. This would stimulate needed research in the field, help to foster ongoing collaborative efforts between universities and public child welfare agencies, and generate much needed relevant data for state and national policies and programs. Experience with such research in various states demonstrates that this can be easily achieved without violating legitimate concerns about confidentiality. In addition, the federal government and private foundations should make funds available to universities and researchers to work with these data sets and address key child welfare and related policy research issues. Researchers that are not solely or largely dependent on state money would then be free to pursue critical issues and present their findings without fear of reprisal.

The federal government is taking the lead in encouraging states to develop comprehensive children's information systems and to collect better data on children in substitute care. This is an important initiative for which the federal government should be applauded. Better data will lead to better research, which, in turn, should result in more cost-effective services and improved treatment for children and families. Again, partnerships with universities could prove to be extremely valuable in facilitating this process because of the expertise universities possess with respect to computer science and the application of technology.

Chapter 2 highlighted some of the problems in evaluating family preservation services. Clearly, more research is needed to see what kinds of family preservation services are most effective and in what circumstances they are more effective than other kinds of children's services. The federal government can help in this area by encouraging states to conduct rigorous evaluations of these services. Also, the national evaluation of family preservation services funded by HHS should prove helpful to practitioners, administrators and elected public officials.

When Speaker of the House Newt Gingrich called for a return to orphanages, the idea was quickly dismissed. It wasn't seriously considered because it was raised by the speaker who was in political hot water due to his excessive partisanship and arrogance and his ethical violations. The idea was also attacked by many in the child welfare field who viewed the concept as a major step backwards. Nevertheless, the reality is that the idea of orphanages is gaining support. For example, the first public residential school for poor inner-city at-risk children opened its door in New Jersey (Children's Academies for Achievement, 1997). Also, the governor of Minnesota has announced an initiative to build several boarding schools for at-risk youth. Both of these developments have the support of prominent academics and child development experts. Like it or not, residential schools for vulnerable children, including abused and neglected children, will probably spread. They are appealing because of the problems confronting public child welfare systems and because of the inability of elected public officials and child welfare administrators to reform them.

In light of this, governors, state legislators, child welfare standard-setting organizations, and other relevant groups should take steps to insure that residential schools meet appropriate operating and child care standards and that they are carefully monitored and evaluated. In addition, policymakers and administrators who support this concept should develop pilot programs and carefully evaluate them before the concept is widely implemented. Until more is know about this concept, it would be unwise to view orphanages or residential schools as the new "silver bullet" or panacea for the growing numbers of troubled and vulnerable children.

Minority Overrepresentation in the Child Welfare System

The overrepresentation of minorities in the child welfare system is a long-standing problem that will continue to plague us until the poverty issue is addressed. In the meantime, far more can and should be done to encourage appropriate kinship placements and adoptions of these children. These children should not be allowed to languish in the child welfare system for years if there is little or no prospect for them being returned to their biological parent or parents.

The Need for an Urban Strategy

Federal child welfare policy and legislation are directed at the states as entities. There are good reasons for this. Child welfare systems are creatures of state governments. It is easier for the federal government to deal with fifty states than it would be to try to work with the many thousands of local units of government (e.g., counties and municipalities) that are in some way involved in child welfare activities across the country. While we recognize the issues involved and generally support a state-level strategy on the part of the federal government, our research indicates that child welfare policies and practices are quite idiosyncratic, even in a state-administered child welfare system such as exists in Michigan.

There are enormous variations in practices and child welfare outcomes among counties in Michigan. The probabilities for reunification, achieving permanency, never achieving permanency, and being initially placed in a costly and restrictive setting should not be dependent upon a child's county of residence. These practices raise serious legal and professional questions that need careful examination by researchers, children's legal scholars, child welfare professionals, child advocates, and national, state, and local elected public officials.

Wayne County, which includes the city of Detroit, accounts for approximately 40 percent of Michigan's entire foster care caseload. Approximately one out of three child welfare cases placed out of their homes in Wayne County involves an infant. Wayne County's child welfare practices and outcomes (e.g., length of time a child is in the system before a permanent placement is made and use of child caring institutions) are among the poorest in the state. This suggests that it might be advisable for child welfare officials in Michigan to consider developing a reform strategy targeted specifically at Wayne County. Likewise, the federal government should consider working in collaboration with appropriate state and local officials on the development of an urban child welfare strategy to help address the unique and desperate needs in large cities. This is not the first time such a recommendation has been made. Kammerman and Kahn (1989) made a similar suggestion after visiting and examining the needs of social service and child welfare agencies in selected.

The federal government's approach to implementing an urban strategy could be similar to our recommendations for addressing the need for state-level reforms. The federal government could have a national competition among urban areas for designation as federally-financed field sites. Sites could be models for testing and evaluating family and children's service reform and service delivery efforts and strategies designed to eradicate child poverty. This could include such things as consolidation and integration of services, restructuring services, development of new services, refinancing, and testing new approaches. It could serve as a catalyst for encouraging a broader conceptualization of service integration (e.g. health, mental health, child welfare, juvenile justice, economic support, housing, education, and neighborhood revitalization) than has been the case to date. Urban areas could even include experimental family preservation programs and/or community parenting centers as part of their proposal to the federal government. Such a strategy should also be linked to universities which are particularly well equipped to conduct evaluations and consider the implications for professional training.

Child Welfare and Delinquency

In chapter 5, we found few cases of children who were in substitute care for reasons of abuse and/or neglect who subsequently committed serious and violent delinquent acts resulting in commitment to the state youth correction system. This is an encouraging finding that can help policymakers better understand the dynamics of substitute care. Other states should explore this phenomenon and see whether they are similar to Michigan's.

The Role of Private Foundations in Child Welfare

Private foundations are an important source of ideas, innovation, and new funding for social welfare programs and research. Foundations are in the unique position of being able to take risks and to promote and encourage experimentation. The role some foundations try to play, particularly in a crucial area like child welfare, is sometimes far more influential than the level of their financial investments. Because of this, they should take care to insure that they are playing a constructive role in policy, program development, research, and in helping to bring about needed change. They should not, as was the case with family preservation, be in the business of selling ill-conceived and untested ideas as if they were the gospel or a panacea.

In the instance of family preservation, the overselling of the program, even in the face of conflicting and credible research, ultimately led to the enactment of new federal legislation (the Family Preservation and Support Act of 1993 and the family preservation component of the Adoption and Safe Families Act of 1997) and the appropriation of $1 billion in federal funds for programs that don't work and that some feel may even be dangerous. More importantly, it also led to many vulnerable children being kept in harm's way. Perhaps if there are appropriate checks and balances within foundations and of foundation board members exercise more oversight and, when appropriate, seek independent counsel and advice about new initiatives proposed by their staff such a problem might be prevented from occurring in the future.

Reunification Issues

Our research suggests that fewer children placed into foster care in Michigan are being reunited with their birth parents than many believed to be the case. Research in California indicates that the rates of reunification in that state are also relatively low. These findings raise serious questions about the concept of reunification that need to be carefully examined. For example, research should be conducted in other jurisdictions to determine exactly what the rates of reunification really are. Also, studies should be conducted to determine what the real prospects for reunification may be. For reasons that are not entirely clear, child welfare workers are not returning nearly as many children placed into foster care to their once abusing and neglectful parents as many had hoped. Are these workers making the right decision? What would it take to increase the rates of reunification without compromising the safety of children? We need to find answers to these questions.

Residential Treatment

A substantial and disproportionate amount of child welfare dollars goes into the care and treatment of children placed into costly group homes, residential treatment centers, and other residential and in-patient programs.

The data from our Michigan study indicates that only 25 percent of the children were successfully discharged from these facilities into society. The other 75 percent were either transferred or discharged to another facility or returned to residential care within one year. Research should be conducted in other states to see whether the findings in Michigan are unique. Residential care and treatment may be the best mode of treatment for some children and should be available when needed. However, more research is needed to determine what kinds of residential treatment are effective with what kinds of children. More importantly, it may be more productive, and less costly, to adopt a different view of the children typically referred to institutional care. Instead of viewing the child as the problem who must be "fixed" in a protected environment, it might be more appropriate to perceive the child as having problems and being in need in help and support but also as a normal human being who responds in an normal and predictable way to abnormal conditions, the abnormal conditions being criminal behavior at the hands of parents. For example, what is perceived in the United States as a status offense (e.g., truancy or incorrigibility) committed by children is defined in other cultures as a parental failure. In these cultures, the focus of intervention is the parents and not the child.

Policy Implications for the State of Michigan

One of the most critical findings from our research is the importance of the very first placement decision. In short, where children are first placed largely determines where they will end their child welfare career. If a child is first put in a permanent placement, the odds are that he or she will end his or her career in such a placement. Likewise, if a child is put in a nonpermanent placement, the chances are that he or she will remain in such a placement. This suggests that if permanency is to continue being a key goal of the child welfare system in Michigan, then every effort should be made to initially place every child in a permanent setting. In instances when a permanent placement is not possible, every effort should be made to place children in a permanent setting within a few (preferably less than six) months. The reason for this is that the chances for achieving permanency dramatically decrease the longer a child is living in a nonpermanent setting.

Our findings indicate that only about one out of every three children placed out of their homes in Michigan are reunited with their parent(s) within four years. We were surprised, frankly, that so few children were reunified within that period of time. While there is much interest in reunification, it is clear that much more needs to be known about this issue. We need to know, for example: Why are so few children reunified with their biological parents in Michigan within four years? Can the proportion of children who are reunited sooner be significantly increased? If so, what needs to be done in order to accomplish this goal? Our findings in Michigan cause us to wonder: How many children are actually being reunified with their parent(s) in other states?

Is the low rate of reunification in Michigan unique?

We were particularly startled with our discovery that over half of all infants placed into substitute care did not achieve permanency before the age of four years. This is also an issue that cries out for further research. We were just as surprised to find that the FIA's records indicate that approximately one-third of all children placed in a nonpermanent setting will never achieve permanency. This represents an extraordinary number of children who are essentially being raised by the government in "permanent foster care." The good news is that 75 percent of these children have only one placement. In other words, the overwhelming majority is not being bounced around from one placement to another. They have a stable living and family like environment. Children who never achieve permanency and who experience more than one placement, however, tend to have several placements. This is of great concern, particularly in light of what others have discovered about the impact of multiple placements on the lives of children and our findings about the potential link between multiple placements and subsequent state commitment for serious delinquent behavior.

While we are encouraged by the stability permanent foster care affords children, there are many issues and questions raised by this practice. For example, why are so many children, particularly infants and toddlers, in permanent foster care? Can some of these children be reunified with their parent(s) or placed with relatives? Why aren't the foster parents of these children adopting them or being made their permanent legal guardians? Why aren't more of these children being adopted in general, particularly the younger (infants and toddlers) children? Also, should the federal government continue to subsidize permanent foster care, and what are the implications for doing so?

The massive rates of recidivism, or the recycling of children in and out of institutions, particularly private not-for-profit group homes and residential treatment centers, needs to be addressed quickly and carefully. At present, residential treatment services appear to be largely feeding off of failure. This is also costing the state of Michigan a great deal of money. It is a situation that, while not the subject of much public discussion, is troubling and of great concern to many public and private child welfare agency professionals. FIA should provide incentives to private not-for-profit agencies to restructure themselves. The emphasis should be on encouraging agencies to divest themselves of providing costly residential treatment and urging them to develop less expensive and less intrusive community-based options.

In addition, FIA should initiate a study to determine precisely how many abused and neglected children may need such treatment in the future and what the nature of the treatment should be. The study should also examine the need for aftercare and transition services. Aftercare and transition services are in short supply and are relatively undeveloped in Michigan. Such a study should be done in collaboration with representatives from the private child welfare community, academics, community health and welfare planning agencies, juvenile court judges, state and local elected public officials, public interest groups, and child advocacy organizations.

Our research also indicates that there are inequities and other serious questions about the adoption process in Michigan. In light of the mandates in the Adoption and Safe Families Act of 1997, FIA should launch an immediate thorough and objective examination into all foster care cases in order to determine those cases where enhanced efforts to achieve permanency, particularly adoption, may be possible. They should consider giving priority and incentives for adoption to current foster parents. In addition, FIA should examine the impact of subsidies on adoption placements. While the number of cases receiving adoption subsidies has steadily increased, there are questions about whether there have been corresponding increases in the number of children being placed for adoption and in the number of adoption confirmations.

Gerald Miller, the former director of the Michigan Family Independence Agency, wrote an editorial in the *Detroit Free Press* about FIA's accomplishments during his tenure there. Among other things, Miller wrote: "The agency will double its investment in prevention, increase its ability to protect children and preserve families, and provide more permanent homes for children who must be removed from their birth parents" (Miller, 1996, October 15). This statement reflects the ambivalence, lack of clear vision, and fundamental dilemmas confronting child welfare agencies today. It indicates that the FIA is still wedded to the faulty logic that equal weight and attention should be given to protecting children and preserving families, no matter how abusive they are. As we have noted earlier, as appealing as this ideology may seem, these are often two fundamentally incompatible goals. The primary mission of public child welfare should be to protect children. If families need services, they should be provided with them but the primary mission must be kept in mind. The editorial was prompted by a perception that FIA had placed the interests of the family above the protection of children.

Another basic problem with the ideology of family preservation advocates is that they rely far more on art than science. The reality is: (1) we don't know which families are amenable to interventions designed to allow them to live together without further abusing and neglecting their children, and (2) we don't know what kinds of interventions are likely to be most effective with abusing and neglectful families. Until we find the answers to these and other basic questions, decisions about whether vulnerable children can be left in their own homes will tend to be made based upon hastily developed and ill-informed agency policies and professional "experience." Decisions made on this basis will undoubtedly lead to further criticism because it is more likely than not that some children will be kept in family environments where they are subject to mistreatment. Consequently, we think FIA would be well advised to launch a new and rigorous study of their Families First program as well as other family preservation and support service programs.

CONCLUSION

Historically, the child welfare system was charged with the responsibility of protecting children and making decisions that were in their best interests. Beginning in the late 1970s and early 1980s, the system took on the added responsibility of strengthening and preserving families. This was a particularly interesting development considering that there was mounting evidence to indicate that the child welfare system was failing to carry out its original mandate.

We are not persuaded that an obsolete, tired, and failing child welfare system can or even should be rejuvenated and take on the added and awesome responsibility of addressing the myriad needs and problems troubled families with vulnerable children in our society are confronting. Instead, we think the time has come to rethink our entire approach to child welfare. The current system should be dismantled and replaced with new and potentially more promising strategies and approaches for meeting the needs of abused and neglected children. At the very least, we should insure that such children are not further victimized by the very system charged with their care and protection. We should also eliminate the practice of having so many of them ending up essentially "being raised by the government."

While we think the existing system can and should be improved, history suggests that policymakers, professionals, and child advocates should be guarded in their expectations. Previous attempts at trying to reform services to abused and neglected children along traditional lines have not accomplished very much. Although Americans do not generally favor or support radical change, it is unlikely that anything short of this will have much of an impact on the child welfare system.

REFERENCES

Bernstein, N. (1997, May 4). Deletion of word in welfare bill opens foster care to big business. *New York Times* p. A1.

Children's Academies for Achievement. (1997). *Our inner-city kids don't ask for much, just a chance.* New York: Children's Academies for Achievement.

Gelles, R. J. (1996). *The book of David.* New York: Basic Books.

Hagedorn, J. M. (1995). *Forsaking our children: Bureaucracy and reform in the child welfare system.* Chicago: Lake View.

Kammerman, S. B., and Kahn, A. J. (1989). *Social services for children, youth and families in the United States.* New York: Annie E. Casey Foundation.

Lerman, P. (1980). Trends and issues in the deinstitutionalization of youths in trouble. *Crime and Delinquency,* 26, 281–98.

Lindsey, D. (1994). *The welfare of children.* New York: Oxford University Press.

Lutz, Lorrie L. and Monica E. Oss. The Kansas Child Welfare Privatization Initiative: A Look One Year Later. *The Children's Vanguard.* February, 1998.

Miller, G. (1996, October 15). Michigan leads in welfare reform. *Detroit Free Press.*

Moynihan, D. P. (1996) *Miles to go: A personal history of social policy.* Cambridge, MA: Harvard University Press.

Osborne, D. (1993). A new federal compact: Sorting out Washington's proper role. In W. Marshal and M. Schram (Eds.), *Mandate for change* (pp. 237–61). New York: Berkeley Publishing Group.

Pelton, L. H. (1991). Beyond permanency planning: Restructuring the public child welfare system. *Social Work, 36,* 337–43.

Pelton, L. H. (1992). A functional approach to reorganizing family and child welfare interventions. *Children and Youth Services Review,* 14, 289–303.

Plotnick, R. D. (1997). Child poverty can be reduced. *The Future of Children,* 7(2), 55–71.

Proceedings and Debates of the 105th Congress, 105th Cong., 1st Sess., Congressional Record 143 (1997).

U.S. General Accounting Office. (1993). Foster care: Services to prevent out-of-home placements are limited by funding barriers (GAO/HRD 93–76). Washington, DC: Government Printing Office.

Index

About the Authors

IRA M. SCHWARTZ is Dean of the School of Social Work at the University of Pennsylvania. He has written numerous articles and books on juvenile justice, including, most recently, *Juvenile Detention: Out of the Closets* (1994) and *Home-based Services for Troubled Children* (1995).

GIDEON FISHMAN, Associate Professor of Sociology at the University of Haifa, is cofounder and codirector of the Minerva Center for Youth Policy at the University. He is the author of numerous articles on crime trends, stereotypes, violent behavior, and suicidal behavior and is coauthor with Arye Rattner of *Justice for All? Jews and Arabs in the Israeli Criminal Justice System* (Greenwood, 1998).

ISBN 0-275-96264-4

9 780275 962647

90000>

EAN

HARDCOVER BAR CODE